ROUTLEDGE LIBRARY EDITION: SYNTAX

Volume 10

THE SYNTAX AND SEMANTICS OF WH-CONSTRUCTIONS

THE SYNTAX AND SEMANTICS OF WH-CONSTRUCTIONS

PAUL HIRSCHBUHLER

LONDON AND NEW YORK

First published in 1985 by Garland Publishing, Inc.

This edition first published in 2017
by Routledge
2 Park Square, Milton Park, Abingdon, Oxon OX14 4RN

and by Routledge
711 Third Avenue, New York, NY 10017

Routledge is an imprint of the Taylor & Francis Group, an informa business

© 1985 Paul Hirschbu?hler

All rights reserved. No part of this book may be reprinted or reproduced or utilised in any form or by any electronic, mechanical, or other means, now known or hereafter invented, including photocopying and recording, or in any information storage or retrieval system, without permission in writing from the publishers.

Trademark notice: Product or corporate names may be trademarks or registered trademarks, and are used only for identification and explanation without intent to infringe.

British Library Cataloguing in Publication Data
A catalogue record for this book is available from the British Library

ISBN: 978-1-138-20096-8
ISBN: 978-1-138-21859-8 (Set)
ISBN: 978-1-315-43729-3 (Set) (ebk)
ISBN: 978-1-138-20091-3 (Volume 10) (hbk)
ISBN: 978-1-315-51353-9 (Volume 10) (ebk)

Publisher's Note
The publisher has gone to great lengths to ensure the quality of this reprint but points out that some imperfections in the original copies may be apparent.

Disclaimer
The publisher has made every effort to trace copyright holders and would welcome correspondence from those they have been unable to trace.

The Syntax and Semantics of Wh-Constructions

Paul Hirschbühler

Garland Publishing, Inc. ■ New York & London
1985

Library of Congress Cataloging-in-Publication Data

Hirschbühler, Paul, 1947–
　The syntax and semantics of wh-constructions.

　(Outstanding dissertations in linguistics)
　Bibliography: p.
　1. Grammar, Comparative and general—Interrogative.
2. Montague grammar.　3. French language—Interrogative.
I. Title.　II. Series.
P299.I57H5　1985　　415　　85-13192
ISBN 0-8240-5449-0 (alk. paper)

© 1985 by Paul Hirschbühler
All rights reserved

The volumes in this series are printed on
acid-free, 250-year-life paper.

Printed in the United States of America

UNIVERSITY
OF SHEFFIELD
LIBRARY

To my parents

ACKNOWLEDGMENTS

I first would like to thank the members of my committee, Emmon Bach, Barbara Hall Partee, Alberto Rivas, and Edwin Williams, for their advice and patience throughout this year.

I owe a special debt to my fellow student Irene Heim, whose constant help made it possible for me to write on the semantics of questions. I also benefited from discussion on several aspects of this dissertation with Elisabeth Engdahl, John Goldsmith, Steve Lapointe, Jean Lowenstamm, and Richard Saenz.

Too many other people helped me in one way or another throughout my studies for me to thank them all here. I would like however to single out Philippe and Claudette Barbaud, Joan Bresnan, Cathy Connors, Marc and Mireille Dominicy, Gilles Fauconnier, Cheryl Goodenough, Helen Goodluck, Collette Dubuisson, Richard Kayne, Roger Higgins, George Lurquin, Judith Mc A'Nulty, Yves-Charles Morin, Hans Obenauer, Paul Pupier, and last but not least Nicolas Ruwet.

Finally, my deepest thanks go to my friends in Amherst and elsewhere in New England, who made this last year here the most pleasant one.

CONTENTS

page

CHAPTER I. INTRODUCTION. 1

CHAPTER II. THE SEMANTICS OF QUESTIONS 5
   2.0 Introduction. 5
   2.1 Questions as Abstraction on the Questioned Phrase . 6
       2.1.1 Informal presentation. 6
       2.1.2 Context variables. 9
       2.1.3 Formalization. 10
   2.2 Problems. 12
       2.2.1 Non wh-quantification in questions 12
       2.2.2 Coordination of questions. 17
             2.2.2.1 Inadequacy of Hausser's analysis. . 17
             2.2.2.2 A solution. 21
             2.2.2.3 Coordination of expressions
                        belonging to different categories . 22
       2.2.3 Embedding of questions 23
       2.2.4 Extensional and intensional interpretation . 24
       2.2.5 Surface non-redundant answers. 26
       2.2.6 Yes-no and alternative questions 28
       2.2.7 Ungrammatical yes-no questions 31
   2.3 Conclusion. 37

CHAPTER III. MULTIPLE QUESTIONS 39
   3.0 Introduction. 39
   3.1 Answers to Multiple Questions 39
   3.2 Towards an Analysis of Multiple Questions . . . 46
   Footnotes. 50

CHAPTER IV. KARTTUNEN'S ANALYSIS OF QUESTIONS. 53
   4.1 General Features of Karttunen's Analysis. . . . 53
       4.1.1 Sets of propositions 53
       4.1.2 True propositions. 54
       4.1.3 The performative analysis. 54

	page
CHAPTER IV.	
4.2 Single and Multiple Questions.	54
Footnotes	57
CHAPTER V. ITERATED MULTIPLE QUESTIONS AND SCOPE AMBIGUITIES.	59
5.0 Introduction	59
5.1 Kuno and Robinson's Analysis and a Modified Version of it.	61
5.2 Evidence for the Ambiguity of Iterated Questions	63
5.2.1 Iterated questions and VP interpretation.	63
5.2.2 Iterated questions and cleft sentences.	74
5.2.3 Ungrammatical narrow scope reading.	76
5.2.4 Wide scope reading "contextually" preferred	77
5.3 Definite NP's and Some Problems.	79
5.4 Iterated Questions and *Whether*	83
Footnotes	89
CHAPTER VI. THE ALTERNATION BETWEEN *QUOI* AND *QUE* IN QUESTIONS IN FRENCH	93
6.0 Introduction	93
6.1 Background	94
6.2 Tensed Clauses	98
6.2.1 Distribution of *quoi* and *que*.	98
6.2.2 The traditional view.	102
6.2.3 Obenauer's analysis	102
6.2.4 Obenauer's arguments.	104
6.2.4.1 Indirect questions	104
6.2.4.2 Restrictiveness.	110
6.2.4.3 *Que* and case	111
6.2.4.4 The *que/qui* alternation in questions	111
6.2.5 *Que* as a pronoun.	112
6.3 Infinitival Clauses.	119
6.3.1 Introduction.	119
6.3.2 QUE and QUOI in main clauses.	119
6.3.3 QUE and QUOI in embedded sentences.	120
6.3.4 Obenauer's analysis	121
6.3.5 Gougenheim's insight.	123

		page
CHAPTER VI.		
	6.3.6 The rules for *que* and *quoi*.	126
	6.3.6.1 Analysis 1	126
	6.3.6.2 Analysis 2	127
	6.3.6.3 Base generation.	127
6.4	Inanimate *qui* in the XVIth-XVIIIth Centuries	128
6.5	Conclusion	129
Footnotes		131
CHAPTER VII. FREE RELATIVES.		139
7.0	Introduction	139
7.1	Free Relatives in French. A Summary	139
7.2	Bresnan and Grimshaw's Analysis.	144
7.3	Evidence for wh in Comp.	145
	7.3.1 Dutch	146
	7.3.2 *Quoi* in free relatives.	147
	7.3.2.1 Wh-phrase in Comp.	148
	7.3.2.2 Wh in the antecedent position.	150
	7.3.3 Montreal French	152
7.4	S versus $\bar{S}$	155
7.5	Pro-PP Heads	159
7.6	A First Conclusion	160
7.7	Free Relatives with Wh in Comp	161
	7.7.1 Ancient Greek	161
	7.7.1.1 Headless relatives	161
	7.7.1.2 Internal head relatives.	163
	7.7.2 XIIth-XVIth century French.	165
	7.7.3 XVIth-XVIIth century Spanish.	166
	7.7.4 Present day Spanish	167
	7.7.5 A correlation?	168
7.8	Infinitival Free Relatives	168
7.9	Conclusion	170
Footnote.		172

	page
CHAPTER VIII. CONCLUSION	173
BIBLIOGRAPHY	177

CHAPTER I

INTRODUCTION

Wh-constructions have been among the constructions most studied by generative grammarians over the last ten years. Within the framework known as the Standard Theory and its extensions, this area of syntax has generated a great deal of theoretical discussion and controversy. The theoretical approach emanating from the work of Chomsky (1973 and after) has been developed in a number of detailed studies, some of the most impressive being Kayne's (1974) and Vergnaud's (1974) analyses of relative clauses in French, Allen's (1977) study of wh-constructions in Old English, and Chomsky and Lasnik's (1977) analysis of relative clauses in English. Relatively little work of importance has been done on the semantics of these constructions in this general framework, Vergnaud (1974) being a notable exception. Most of the semantic studies of relative clauses and questions have been done by philosophers and by linguists working in formal semantics, in particular by those working in the framework of Montague grammar.

Most people working within the transformational tradition reject or ignore the semantic theory put forward by Montague, and most people working in Montague's semantic framework don't use a standard transformational approach in their syntactic analyses. Yet it is quite possible to do work within a theory that would have a syntactic component of one of the kinds of transformational grammars, and a semantic component of the kind advocated by Montague; Partee (1975), Bach (1977), Cooper (1975), Cooper and Parsons (1976), and especially McCloskey (1978) are good examples of this. Since a primary goal of linguistic theory is the explication of the relationship between the semantic interpretation of sentences and their structural (syntactic) properties, such attempts to relate syntactic and semantic analysis in a precise way are clearly of great potential importance. The fruitfulness of such an integrated approach will depend in part on the detail and accuracy of both the syntactic and semantic analyses under consideration. Sometimes the main syntactic aspects of some constructions are well understood, but the semantic ones are not, sometimes the opposite is true. Once we have a clear idea of the correct syntactic representation for a construction that we want to be mapped into a semantic representation, as well as what the semantic representation should be like, we are in a good position to evaluate better the hypotheses that have been put forward about how to associate syntactic and semantic representations of sentences and modify these hypotheses in whatever way seems to be required. Further, the attempt to arrive at an integrated semantic and syntactic analysis of a given construction may lead us to revise the syntactic or semantic analysis from which we began.

The studies found in this dissertation are detailed analyses of aspects of the semantics and the syntax of some wh-constructions, and they should be considered as a contribution to the studies concentrating on particular aspects of wh-constructions that are necessary, together with the more theoretically oriented work, in our attempt to develop a linguistic theory that accounts both for the syntax and the semantics of natural languages.

The dissertation is organized as follows.

The first part, from Chapter II to V deals with the semantics of questions. The second part, Chapter VI and VII, discusses the syntax of *que* and *quoi* (what) in questions in French and the syntax of free relatives in French and other languages.

In Chapter II, I examine an analysis of questions based on the view that a question and a non-redundant answer together form a sentence, i.e. an expression which has a truth-value. The most explicit analysis adopting this point of view, and the one whose predictions are the clearest, is that developed by Hausser and Zaefferer (1976) and Hausser (1978) in the framework of Montague Grammar. Our discussion is based on their analysis. We study the predictions made by their analysis for types of questions they didn't consider or they didn't consider in detail and see how some difficulties that arise can be overcome.

In the third chapter, devoted to multiple questions, we first try to establish clearly what sorts of answers are appropriate to multiple questions, i.e. what the facts that have to be accounted for are; we then see how the analysis discussed in Chapter II can account for the fact that (1)b and (1)c are possible answers to (1)a, where each wh-phrase is in the singular:

(1) a. Which boy likes which girl?

    b. Fred likes Sue and Paul likes Muriel.

    c. Fred likes Sue.

The fourth chapter is a short review of the central aspects of Karttunen's (1977a,b) analysis of questions and we point out a problem that his analysis faces, i.e. his analysis predicts that while (1)c is an appropriate possible answer to (1)a, (1)b is not.

The fifth chapter discusses iterated multiple questions like (2),

(2) Who knows where we bought what?

and I present new and clear evidence supporting the usually held view, challenged by Kuno and Robinson (1972), that such questions are ambiguous.

Chapter VI is a discussion of the alternation between *que* and *quoi* (what) in questions in French, and I argue that *que* in questions is an interrogative pronoun, and not, as argued by Obenauer (1976, 1977) the complementizer *que*. Part of the material discussed in this chapter is taken up again in Chapter VII.

In Chapter VII, I discuss the syntax of free relatives with respect to the question of whether the wh-phrase in this construction occupies the antecedent position, in which case the wh-phrase is not part of the relative clause itself, or the complementizer position, in which case it is part of the relative clause. Until Bresnan (1973) challenged that view, it was assumed without discussion that the wh-phrase in free relatives was part of the embedded clause, which is clearly the case for languages like Classical Greek, Old and Middle French. I have argued (1976a,b) that in French today the wh-phrase occupies the antecedent position, something that Bresnan (1973), Allen (1977), Grimshaw (1977), Daalder (1977), and Bresnan and Grimshaw (1978) argued was the case for the free relatives or a subset of them in the languages they examined. It is claimed that the central argument in favor of that hypothesis has lost most of its force, given some facts of Dutch discussed by Van Riemsdijk (1978), and additional facts from different varieties of French are presented which fit better with the analysis where the wh-phrase in free relatives occupies the Complementizer position. Facts from a variety of languages are discussed which show that free relatives provide a rich area for much more research.

CHAPTER II

THE SEMANTICS OF QUESTIONS

2.0 Introduction

Many logical analyses of questions have been proposed in recent years. One aspect common to all of them is that they try to formalize the relation that exists between a question and a possible or true answer to it. Analyses have however diverged on what they took as an answer. Decisions on what counts as an answer to a question lead to different analyses. This can be seen by comparing, for example, Hintikka (1974, 1976), Karttunen (1977a,b), and Hausser and Zaefferer (1976).

Considering first the linguistic literature, one sees that questions are regarded as a member of a family of constructions. Members of this family include: direct and indirect questions, headed and headless relatives, cleft and pseudo-cleft sentences. Although these are different constructions, they have common properties in many languages. Let us limit ourselves to questions and relative clauses. Considering English and French, for example, the obvious similarities have to do with the existence of wh-movement, which appears to work somewhat differently in the four constructions (see Postal, 1971) and with the wh-words found in these constructions. As far as the distribution of wh-words is concerned, questions, and especially embedded questions in French (see for example the distribution of *que/quoi*, chapters VI and VII), are more similar to headless relatives than any of them is to headed relatives. Looking at other languages, one often finds that the relative words found in headed relatives, if any, are systematically different from those found in questions, which match more or less those found in free relatives. This is for example the case in Navajo, 'where free relatives are indistinguishable from a kind of indirect question, both being different from other kinds of relatives' (Andrews, 1976:65), or in German or Dutch where 'w-words' are found in questions and free relatives but not in headed relatives. See also Cooper (1978) for Chinese for example, and Keenan and Hull (1973b) for examples from a variety of languages. Those similarities between questions and, in varying proportions, headed and headless relatives are probably not accidental, and I believe it is more important to focus at the beginning on the similarities than on the differences that exist. If we assume that the relative clause itself in headless and headed relatives, i.e. what is dominated by $\bar{S}$ in Chomsky's framework, receives the same sort of translation in the semantics, then the differences with respect to the modalities of application of wh-movement (if wh-movement is each time involved; see chapter VII)

and in the choice of wh-words used in each construction should be
of no importance as far as logical structure is concerned. And
the surface similarities between free relatives and questions suggest,
at least as a reasonable working hypothesis, that their semantics,
up to a certain point, could be similar. We assume that they are
similar, and this assumption has led us to focus especially on one
type of analysis of questions that allows for maximal similarity,
though we will not limit ourselves to discussing only one approach.

Although the number of analyses of questions is rather large,
we will talk only about three analyses, and especially two of them.

The first one is found, in different forms, in Egli (1973, 1974,
1976), Hull (1974, 1975), Hull and Keenan (1973a, 1973b), Hausser and
Zaefferer (1976), and Hausser (1978); other people probably have suggested the same approach. Our discussion will be based mainly on
Egli, Hausser and Zaefferer, and Hausser. In the course of our
discussion of ungrammatical yes-no questions (in 2.2.7) a few words
will be said about the second analysis, that which Hausser proposes
for indirect questions, and it will be rejected. The third analysis
discussed will be that proposed by Karttunen (1977a,b), who builds
on some earlier work by Hamblin (1973). Most of our efforts have
been devoted to the first analysis; I find the analysis attractive,
and it is crucial to know what its strong and weak points are:
this is what we have tried to make clear. I will not go into Karttunen's analysis in much detail here and therefore will not try to
draw definite conclusions about the respective merits of the approach
defended by Egli and others and that proposed by Karttunen.

2.1 Questions as abstraction on the questioned phrase

2.1.1 Informal presentation.

Egli, Hull, Keenan, Hausser, and Zaefferer propose that a question
and an answer to it be considered as equivalent to a sentence. So,
(a) in the examples below is considered as equivalent to (b): a question-
answer pair is equivalent to an assertion (an ordinary declarative
sentence).

(1) a. Who came? Peter.

b. Peter came.

(2) a. When did he leave? Yesterday.

b. He left yesterday.

(3) a. Is Fred here? No.

b. Fred isn't here.

The relevant answers are what Hausser and Zaefferer (1976:5) cal
minimal, non-redundant answers. We will take an analysis of question:
based on this approach as the basis for most of our discussion and we
will see what problems such an analysis raises as well as what its
attractive features are.

The formalization that we will build on was first proposed by Egli (1973), who proposed representing questions by using the lambda operator to bind the variable corresponding to the questioned phrase. In his system, the dialogue (1)a is represented by (4):

(4) $?\lambda s[s\ came] \vdash Peter$

where '?' is the question performative, '⊢' the assertion performative, and 's' is a variable of the type of an NP. The wh-clause itself, translated as in (5)a, denotes the class of possible denotations of NP's which taken as the interpretation of s in (5)b makes it true.

(5) a. $\lambda s\ [s\ came]$

     b. s came

(6), the translation of (1)b, is equivalent to (4):

(6) $\lambda s[s\ came]\ (Peter)$

How a question and an answer form a sentence in a dialogue is perhaps more conspicuously shown in (7), adapted from Egli (1974: 121), where among other things we have replaced the δ-operator by the λ-operator (for the difference, see Egli (1973:368)):

(7)

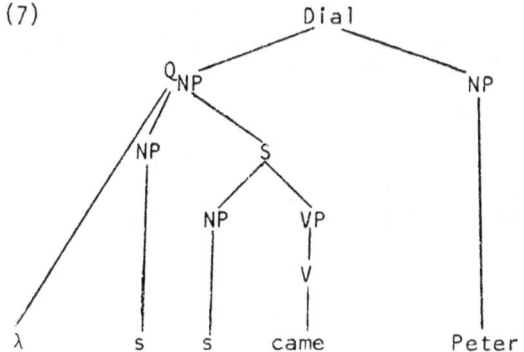

An answer to a question is thus an expression of the same category as the variable that is bound by the λ-operator. We will come back to this later.

Such an analysis seems to have the two desired features mentioned in the introduction.

First it makes the relation between a question and a possible or true answer very clear. One can see a question as denoting a set by one of its defining properties, and an answer as being a specification of its members. This analysis allows for any of (8)a-c to be counted as an answer to the question in (1)a:

(8) a. Peter, Paul, and Mary.

     b. The people I told you about yesterday.

     c. Every man.

     d. The people who came.

(8)d provides no information and wouldn't count as a satisfactory answer, while (8)a-c are all potentially satisfactory answers. I am not sure whether the specification of when a true answer is a satisfactory answer should be part of the semantics of questions itself, as argued by Hintikka (1974, 1976) or whether it should be part of the pragmatics. I tend to give preference to the second of these views. For a discussion of this, besides Hintikka, I refer the reader to Hull (1974).

The second interesting aspect of this approach is that it makes it easy to relate questions and relative clauses: a question is similar to a step in the derivation of a relative clause, though there are differences here in the choice of variables. For example, the CN phrase in (9) is derived as in (10):

(9) man who came.

(10) a. *man* translates as: man'

b. *who came* translates as: $\lambda x [came'(x)]$

c. *man who came* translates as: $\lambda y [man'(y) \& \lambda x [came'(x)](y)]$, which is equivalent to (10)d

d. $\lambda y [man'(y) \& came'(y)]$

The wh-clause is translated as an abstract, whether we have questions, headed or headless relatives. In the case of free relatives, assuming that *what* in (11) is in Comp position, we may have the derivation given in (11) for it:

(11) what you read

(12) a. [what you read] translates as $\lambda x [-animate'(x) \& you\ read\ x]$
$\overline{S}$

b. [[what you read]] translates as
NP $\overline{S}$

$\hat{P} \Lambda y [\lambda x [-animate'(x) \& you\ read\ x](y) \rightarrow P\{y\}]$

which is equivalent to:

(12) c. $\hat{P} \Lambda y [[-animate'(y) \& you\ read\ y] \rightarrow P\{y\}]$

That is, we assume that the semantic rule corresponding to the formation of the NP will introduce the translation of *every* (or of the definite article in some cases perhaps), and the translation of the

free relative will be its argument. This is only to suggest one
possible approach to free relatives, and is not intended as anything
close to a definite analysis.

What is left unexplained with this is why wh-words aren't
exactly the same for all three constructions. Some of the differences
will be explained in terms of notions like 'definiteness', headed
relatives not accepting indefinite wh-words as *what*, generally.
Some of the differences between questions and free relatives will
be due to the extra quantification necessary for free relatives,
quantification which sometimes has a surface reflex, e.g. *-ever* in
English. For other differences, we don't envisage any synchronic
explanation. Those differences in themselves are not alarming. To
see this it is only necessary to remember that headed relatives can
appear under a variety of forms in the same language or in different
dialects of a single language, so, we may have a wh-word, or simply
a gap, or a resumptive pronoun and no wh-word:

(13) a. the man who you think came is not here

     b. the man you think came is not here

     c. the man that you think that he came is not here

Those differences have led people to think that in those three
cases the relative clauses will receive different translations.
Similarly, it is not necessarily the case that the differences in
the choice of wh-words available for questions, headed relatives, and
headless relatives imply differences in the sort of translation given
to the wh-clause itself.

We will now look more closely at the formal analysis as developed
by Hausser and Zaefferer (1976) and Hausser (1978), at the problems
it raises once we take into account different kinds of questions that
they did not consider.

2.1.2 Context variables

A non-redundant answer to a question, just like a redundant one,
may be right or wrong, and may be considered as expressing a true
or a false proposition. (15)a is a non-redundant answer to (14)
while (15)b is a redundant answer (for more discussion, see Hausser
and Zaefferer (1976:3-7) and Hausser (1978: 198-202)):

(14) Who came?

(15) a. Peter.

     b. Peter came.

One way to capture this is to consider both redundant and non-redundant answers as expressions of category/type t. The minimal answer in (15)a is an NP (a Term Phrase) however, i.e. an expression of category $t/(t/e)$. Hausser and Zaefferer propose representing a non-redundant answer as the combination of a context-variable and a minimal answer; here we reserve the expression minimal answer to designate the surface expression, for example that in (15)a. The context-variable and the minimal answer put together are taken as forming an expression of category/type t. So, taking Γ as the context-variable and X as a variable over categories to which the minimal answers may belong, a non-redundant answer may be generated by a rule like (16):

(16) S → Γ X

Γ is replaced in the interpretation by the translation of a question occurring in the discourse. I refer the reader to Hausser and Zaefferer (1976:8-11) and Hausser (1978:209-213 and 223-225) for technical details and discussions.

2.1.3. Formalization.

Wh-phrases are treated as expressions containing a free variable or, to simplify, as sorted variables when possible. Who, for example, an NP, i.e. an expression of category t/IV, which corresponds to the type of $^{\vee}P$, is translated as (17) in Hausser and Zaefferer, and as (18), with a sorted variable, in Hausser:

(17) who_n : $\hat{P}P_n\{\hat{x}[human'(x) \, \& \, P\{x\}]\}$, or

$\hat{P}^{\vee}P_n(\hat{x}[human'(x) \, \& \, P\{x\}])$

(18) : $^{\vee}P_n$

The free variable, which will be bound by the lambda-operator in a question must be of the type of the minimal answer, not necessarily of the type of the intension of the wh-word itself. So, in (17) and (18) the free variable is of the type of the intension of a Term-phrase and the wh-word is a Term-phrase, but in (19) the free variable is of the type of the intension of a Term-phrase (category t/IV) while the wh-word itself is of the type of a determiner, i.e. that corresponding to an expression of category T/CN.

(19) which $student_n$: $\hat{P}^{\vee}P_n(\hat{x}[student'(x) \, \& \, P\{x\}])$

This is so in order that the minimal answer corresponds to the variable abstracted upon in the question. We can now turn to the question of why the variable abstracted upon is of the type of the intension of the minimal answer. The intension is taken because Γ, the context-variable, is a function that takes as argument the intension of the minimal answer, in accordance with the general schema for rules of functional application:

(20) If $\alpha \in P_{A/B}$ and $\beta \in P_B$, and α,β translate into α',β' respectively, then $F_k(\alpha,\beta)$ translates into $\alpha'(^\wedge\beta')$.

The variables used must then be of the type of the intension of the minimal answer. The dialogue given in (21) can then be represented by (22):

(21) Who came? John.

(22) a. $\lambda P[\lambda P(^\wedge come')]$

b. $\Gamma \hat{P} P\{^\wedge j\}$

Replacing the context-variable by the translation of the preceding question, we get (23)a, which is equivalent to (23)b. Non-redundant answers are thus equivalent to redundant ones.

(23) a. $\lambda P[\ [^\vee P(^\wedge come')]\ \hat{P} P\{^\wedge j\}$

b. $come'_*(j)$

Two last features of Hausser and Zaefferer's analysis must be mentioned before we start the discussion.

First, there will not only be questions of as many different categories as there are categories of questioned phrases, but also as there are different categories of multiple questions and iterated multiple questions (see chapters III and V). For example, we have the following questions with the corresponding category:

(24)   a.   Who came?   t/T

       b.   Where did he go?   t/IAV

       c.   Who bought what?   (t/T)/T

       etc.

Second, they derive direct questions directly, i.e. they reject the performative analysis (Hausser and Zaefferer, 1976:23), Hausser (1978:203-206), which is the one generally adopted in formal semantics:

see Aqvist (1975), Hintikka (1974, 1976), Egli (1973), and Karttunen (1977a,b).

These two aspects will be discussed in a moment.

2.2 Problems

In the following sections we examine several problems that arise if Hausser and Zaefferer's analysis is adopted without modifications.

2.2.1 Non wh-quantification in questions.

The first and perhaps the most important problem arises with questions like (25):

(25) a. What grade does every student deserve?

b. What is every rock made of?

These questions are ambiguous with respect to the relative scope of the questioned phrase and that of the other quantified phrase (see Keenan and Hull (1973:446), Aqvist (1975:V), and Karttunen (1977b:31-33)). (25)a has for example the following two paraphrases and possible answers:

(26) a. What is the unique grade such that every student deserves it?

b. (a) B.

(27) a. For every student, what grade does he deserve?

b. Bill deserves (a)B, Fred (a)C, and John (an)A.

There is no problem in deriving the first reading. We may assume that the wh-phrase is generated in place and that the introduction of the lambda which binds the free variable in the translation of the wh-phrase is the correlate of some syntactic rule, for example wh-movement, or, if we decide to quantify in all the wh-phrases, we may write up the rule of wh-quantification in such a way that it will put in the lambda as part of the application of the rule, just as Karttunen's rule of wh-quantification(1977b) is a complex operation that combines the sort of translation associated to quantification rules with whatever is necessary to get the translation of a wh-question (compare Karttunen, 1977a and 1977b). Let us just assume here that the wh-phrase is quantified in and the non-wh-quantified phrase is not (whatever combination is tried with respect to the interaction between the wh-quantified phrase and the other, the outcome will always be the same, because of the binding by lambda). Then (25)a will be translated as (28)a, which is finally equivalent to (28)g:

(28) a. $\lambda P \hat{P}^\vee P \, (\hat{x}_o [\text{grade}'(x_o) \, \& \, P\{x_o\}] (\hat{x}_1 [\hat{P} \Lambda x_2 [\text{student}'(x_2) \rightarrow P\{x_2\}] \, (^\wedge \text{deserve}' \, (\hat{P} \, P\{x_1\} \,))])$

b. $\lambda P P^\vee P (\hat{x}_o [\text{grade}'(x_o) \, \& \, P\{x_o\}\,]) (\hat{x}_1 (\Lambda x_2 [\text{student}'(x_2) \rightarrow (^\wedge \text{deserve}' \, (\hat{P} \, P\{x_1\}\,)) \, \{x_2\} \,]])$ by lambda-conversion.

c. $\lambda P P^\vee P (\hat{x}_o [\text{grade}'(x_o) \, \& \, P\{x_o\}\,]) (\hat{x}_1 [\Lambda x_2 [\text{student}'(x_2) \rightarrow (\text{deserve}' \, (\hat{P} \, P\{x_1\}\,)) (x_2)]])$ by brace-convention and down-up cancellation.

d. $\lambda P^\vee P (\hat{x}_o [\text{grade}'(x_o) \, \& \, \hat{x}_1 [\Lambda x_2 [\text{student}'(x_2) \rightarrow \text{deserve}'(\hat{P} \, P\{x_1\}\,) \, (x_2))]]\{x_o\}\,])$ by lambda-conversion

e. $\lambda P^\vee P (\hat{x}_o [\text{grade}'(x_o) \, \& \, \hat{x}_1 [\Lambda x_2 [\text{student}'(x_2) \rightarrow \text{deserve}'(x_2, \hat{P} \, P\{x_1\}\,)]]\{x_o\}\,])$ by Relation Notation.

f. $\lambda P^\vee P (\hat{x}_o [\text{grade}'(x_o) \, \& \, \Lambda x_2 [\text{student}'(x_2) \rightarrow \text{deserve}'(x_2, \hat{P} \, P\{x_o\}\,)]])$ by brace convention, down-up cancellation, and lambda-conversion.

If we apply (28)g to the translation of the minimal answer a(B) -- which, for the sake of discussion, we will assume is translated as $\hat{P} \, P\{^\wedge b\}$ -- we obtain:

(29) $\lambda P^\vee P (\hat{x}_o [\text{grade}'(x_o) \, \& \, \Lambda x_2 [\text{student}'(x_2) \rightarrow \text{deserve}'(x_2, \hat{P} P\{x_o\}\,)]]) (\hat{P} \, P\{^\wedge b\}\,)$

which finally is equivalent to (30):

(30) $\text{grade}'(^\wedge b) \, \& \, \Lambda x_2 [\text{student}'(x_2) \rightarrow \text{deserve}'(\, x_2, \hat{P} P\{^\wedge b\}\,)]$

This corresponds to the intended meaning of (26)b.

Turning now to the other reading of (25)a, paraphrased in (27)a, which allows for each student having a different grade, we can see that it is impossible to obtain the right meaning if we don't abandon Hausser's hypothesis that direct questions are not derived from indirect questions. For example, suppose that we try to quantify in *every student* in (31)a, where question formation has already applied, and whose translation is given in (31)b:

(31) a. What grade does he_2 deserve?

   b. $\lambda P^{\vee} P(\hat{x}_o [grade'(x_o) \& deserve'(x_2, \hat{P}P\{x_o\})])$

To quantify in *every student* in (31)a, which is of category t/T, we need a rule of quantification like (32):

(32) If $\alpha \in P_T$ and $\eta \in P_{t/T}$, then $F_{246,n}(\alpha, \eta) \in P_{t/T}$, where...

[the '...' stands for what follows 'where' in the first rule of quantification in PTQ, S_{14}]

translation: If $\alpha \in P_T, \eta \in P_{t/T}$, and α, η translate into α', η' respectively, then $F_{246,n}(\alpha, \eta)$ translates into

$\lambda P \alpha' (\hat{x}_n [\eta' (P)])$.

If we apply this rule to quantify in *every student* in (31)a, we get (25)a, with the translation of (33)a, which is equivalent to (33)b, which itself is equivalent to (28)g, i.e. (33)b and (28)g denote the same set.

(33) a. $\lambda P_\wedge [\hat{P} \wedge x_1 [stud'(x_1) \rightarrow P\{x_1\}]](\hat{x}_2 [\lambda P^{\vee} P(\hat{x}_o [grade'(x_o) \&$

   $deserve'(x_2, \hat{P} P\{x_o\})])P_\wedge])$

   b. $\lambda P_\wedge [\wedge x_1 [stud'(x_1) \rightarrow {}^{\vee} P_\wedge (\hat{x}_o [grade'(x_o) \& deserve'$

   $(x_1, \hat{P}P\{x_o\})])]]$

(33)b picks out a set of grades and every student deserves the grades contained in that set; with an appropriate treatment of the singular, it should come out that there is only one grade in that set. The point is that there is one set of grades only and that we don't get the desired reading. One may then try to modify the translation rule in (32) and replace it by (34) which is not well-formed in the existing logics.

(34) If $\alpha \in P_T$ and $\eta \in P_{t/T}$, and α, η translate into α', η' respectively, then $F_{246,n}(\alpha, \eta)$ translates into $\alpha'(\hat{x}_n[\eta'])$

Using this to quantify in *every student* in (31)a, we would get (35), which is also not well-formed:

(35) $\Lambda x[\text{student}'(x) \rightarrow \lambda P^{\vee}P(\hat{y}[\text{grade}'(y) \ \& \ \text{deserve}'(\ x, \hat{P}P\{y\} \ )])]$

Such an approach to the problem is consequently incorrect, unless one is ready to develop a new system in which (34) and (35) are well-formed; I don't think this is worth trying at the moment, since there exists another solution. One interesting feature of (35) is that it tries to express that for every student something obtains, which is what the next solution does too. The only thing that is necessary is to assume that direct questions are derived from something like indirect ones, for example with the help of a performative operator, say '?', which, following Karttunen (1977b:9-10) would be interpreted by a suitable meaning postulate which would make it similar to something like 'I ask you to tell me'. This operator would have to be of a variable category so that it can combine with questions of different categories to give an expression of type t. (One may think that this would create a problem for the question-answer pairs: we just need to ensure that only what follows the translation of '?' is substituted for the context variable that is part of the non-redundant answer.) What we can do then to get the reading of (25)a paraphrased in (27)a is simply to quantify in *every student* after the performative operator and (31)a have been put together, i.e. *every student* is quantified in into (36), of category t, by S14 of PTQ. The translation is given in (37), where we have left '?' uninterpreted to save space: I assume Karttunen's interpretation.

(36) ?What grade does he deserve?

(37) a. $\hat{P}\Lambda x[\text{st}'(x) \rightarrow P\{x\}](\hat{y}[?(\hat{P}^{\vee}P(\hat{z}[\text{grade}'(z) \ \& \ \text{deserve}'$

$(\ y, \hat{P}P \ \{z\} \ )])])])$

b. $\Lambda x[\text{st}'(x) \rightarrow \hat{y}[?(\hat{P}^{\vee}P(\hat{z}[\text{grade}'(z) \ \& \ \text{deserve}'$

$(\ y, \ \hat{P}P \ \{z\} \ )])])] \ \{x\} \ ]$

(37) c. $\Lambda x[\text{st}'(x) \rightarrow [?(\hat{P}^{\vee}P(\hat{z}[\text{grade}'(z) \text{ \& deserve}'$
$(x, \hat{P}P \{z\})]))]]$

by brace-convention, down-up cancellation, and
lambda conversion.

What we obtain is clear: when *every student* has widest scope,
we create a set of (direct) questions. For example, if there are
three students, say a,b, and c, we get the three following questions:

(38) a. $\text{St}_*^!(a) \rightarrow ?(\hat{P}\ ^{\vee}P\ (\hat{z}[\text{grade}'(z) \text{ \& deserve}'(^a, \hat{P}P \{z\})]))$

b. $\text{St}_*^!(b) \rightarrow ?(\hat{P}\ ^{\vee}P\ (\hat{z}[\text{grade}'(z) \text{ \& deserve}'(^b, PP \{z\})]))$

c. $\text{St}_*^!(c) \rightarrow ?(\hat{P}\ ^{\vee}P\ (\hat{z}[\text{grade}'(z) \text{ \& deserve}'(^c, PP \{z\})]))$

Each of the questions on the right of the arrow is independent
of the others and allows for a different answer, for example that
given in (27)b. If questions are interpreted as lambda-expressions
of some sort, either of the sort examined here, or of the one proposed
by Karttunen (1977a,b), then questions like (25)a with the interpretation just discussed provide a new and interesting sort of argument
for the performative analysis, the credit for which must be given to
Karttunen (1977a: 33). More generally independently of whether the
performative approach will finally turn out to be correct or not,
the problem just discussed illustrates the necessity of having a
precise interpreted language for the semantics: without that one may
think it is possible to give *every student* widest scope in (25)a by
simply quantifying it in into (31)a for example, which as far as I see,
is equivalent to the way May (1977: 143) treats these readings in
his dissertation (fn. 9, p. 142-146). For example, he assigns (39)a,
which is ambiguous, the logical forms (39)b and (39)c; (39)b is
intended to represent the case where the wh-phrase has wider scope,
while (39)c is intended to represent the case where *each senator* has
wider scope (we have corrected some typo's in May's (vi), our (39)b):

(39) a. What did each senator say?

b. $[_{\overline{S}}[_{Comp}\text{what}]_t\ [_S[\text{each senator}]_\alpha\ [_S\text{did }\alpha\text{ say t}]]]$

c. $[_{\overline{S}}[_{Comp}t]_t\ [_S[\text{each senator}]_\alpha\ [_S[\text{what}]_t\ [_S\text{did }\alpha\text{ say t}]]]]$

But without some interpretation given to quantifiers, wh-phrases, and
questions, it is impossible to figure whether (39)b and c will lead to
the intended interpretations.

A theory of logical form without a parallel theory of interpretation is then in principle inadequate. It is only after we try to account for the ambiguity of (39)a and (25)a is an interpreted system that we may have a chance to see what problems may arise. The specific scope problem we have discussed will arise, I think, in any semantic analysis of questions. Although problematic in some respects, the performative analysis offers at least the advantage of allowing an account of the ambiguity discussed.

Let us turn now to another problem that arises within the sort of analysis examined here.

2.2.2 Coordination of questions.

2.2.2.1 Inadequacy of Hausser's analysis.

We have seen in 1.1.3 that different sorts of questions belong to different categories and types. This is put very clearly in Hausser (1978:212):

> Since we define a direct question and a suited non-redundant answer in such a way that they fit together semantically, the type of the constituents of a class of non-redundant answers (suited with respect to the question in question) *determines the type* of the question. It follows that different kinds of questions have different types.

The problem we face at this point is how it is possible to conjoin questions of different types, as in (40):

(40) When did John leave and what did he take?

The first conjunct, under Hausser's analysis, is of category t/IAV and the second of category t/T. It is generally assumed that one can only conjoin phrases of the same category, i.e. it shouldn't be possible to conjoin a phrase of category t/IAV with a phrase of category t/T. Hausser (1978:219) offers the following with respect to that problem:

> To formally conjoin several direct questions by means of sentential operators is no problem in the kind of λ-calculus employed here. Our concept of an open-L sentence ... will greatly facilitate the derivation of conjoined questions...

Hausser doesn't actually show how he would derive questions like (40). It is certainly not by conjoining already formed questions. The solution he must have in mind is most probably the following one:

(41) 1. Conjoin open-L sentences (Open-L sentences are the syntactic correlate of an open formula and are of category t (Hausser, (1978:220-221)), i.e. conjoin (i) and (ii):

(i) John leaves when$_o$.

(ii) He took what$_1$ with him.

2. After conjoining is done, apply the rule that forms direct questions out of open-L sentences. Let us assume that the syntactic part of the rule would perform wh-movement (and perhaps subject-aux inversion in direct questions) and thus move the wh-phrase of each clause to the front of its own clause. Semantically, the λ's that will be introduced and bind the appropriate variables will have scope over both clauses, so that the conjoined phrases will be of the same type. Using a_n^t as a sorted variable of type <s,f(IAV)>, with *when*$_n$ translated as $^va_n^t$ and $^v P$ for *what*, (40) can be represented as in (iii), ignoring tense and assuming, for convenience, that the wh-phrases are not quantified in:

(iii) $\lambda P \lambda a^t [(j*(a^t (^\wedge leave'))) \ \& \ (j*(^\wedge take'(P)))]$

At first sight this may seem a reasonable way to handle the problem, but it is possible to show that it is not. It is generally assumed that a wh-phrase moved in Comp has scope only over the sentence that it commands. It is also generally assumed, and we will come back to this in Chapter V, that unmoved wh-words may have the same scope as other wh-words moved in Comp's that command them. See for example Chomsky (1973:283-4). Consider now the following sentence:

(42) *Which boy touched which car and which girl did too?

The VP in the second conjunct is missing. The ungrammaticality of (42) can be explained given Williams' (1977) analysis of VP interpretation only under the standard assumptions about the scope of wh-phrases, i.e. only if representations like (iii) in (41) are not allowed. To see this, let us assume that $^v P_1$ is a variable for *which boy*, $^v P_2$ for *which car*, and $^v P_3$ for *which girl*. If we allow

representations like (iii) in (41), (42) could be represented by
(43), with a missing VP in the second conjunct (we have departed
from Williams by not giving internal structure to the empty VP;
nothing hinges on that here; see Sag (1976) for a variant with VP
deletion and Flynn (1978) for a first attempt at an interpretive
account in Montague's framework along the same general lines as
Williams.).

(43) $\lambda P_3 \lambda P_2 \lambda P_1 [[^{\vee}P_1(^{\wedge}\text{touch}'(P_2))] \& [^{\vee}P_3(\underline{\hspace{2cm}})]]$

Assume then that there is a rule copying the translation of the first
VP into the empty slot in the second conjunct (see Williams, 1977:
114 sqq and Flynn, 1978:31-34): this gives us (44), which is well-
formed.

(44) $\lambda P_3 \lambda P_2 \lambda P_1 [[^{\vee}P_1(^{\wedge}\text{touch}'(P_2))] \& [^{\vee}P_3(^{\wedge}\text{touch}'(P_2))]]$

We might thus expect (42) to be grammatical but it is not. We
agree with Chomsky (1973), Hankamer (1974), Karttunen (1977a,b) and
others that a moved wh-phrase has only scope over the sentence that
it commands and that in the semantic representation the λ binding
the variable has scope only over the same sentence that the moved
wh-phrase commands. Similarly, we assume that unmoved wh-phrases
have scope over the same sentence as the moved wh-phrase that commands
them (see references cited above), and that the λ's binding the
variables corresponding to unmoved wh-phrases have scope over the same
sentence as the λ associated with the moved wh-word that commands
them (this says nothing about the relative scope of moved and unmoved
wh-words or of the lambdas associated with each of them). Then (42)
could be represented by (45):

(45) $[[\lambda P_2 \lambda P_1 [^{\vee}P_1(^{\wedge}\text{touch}'(P_2))]] \& [\lambda P_3 [^{\vee}P_3(\underline{\hspace{2cm}})]]]$

After VP-copying we have (46):

(46) $[[\lambda P_2 \lambda P_1 [^{\vee}P_1(^{\wedge}\text{touch}'(P_2))]] \& [\lambda P_3 [^{\vee}P_3(^{\wedge}\text{touch}'(P_2))]]]$

This time the occurence of P_2 in the second conjunct isn't bound,
since it is not in the scope of λP_2, which is buried in the first
conjunct. We may then think of excluding (46) on the ground that it
contains an unbound variable, the P_2 in the second conjunct, on the
model of Williams who assumes that several sentences with empty
VP's which he discusses are ungrammatical because their logical form
contains an unbound variable (or trace) after his VP copying rule

has applied: a logical form containing an unbound variable is semantically anomalous (see Williams, 1977:121,131,135,136).

As such this restriction is too strong since one might expect P_2 to be interpretable with respect to the context. A less general restriction would be to say that copied-in variables may not be interpreted pragmatically with respect to the context. Notice that if the second occurrence of P_2 in (46) could be interpreted pragmatically with respect to the context it would anyway not give the interpretation that we are discussing, i.e. that in which the second conjunct is also interpreted as a multiple question: it would be interpreted in the same way as *it/him/her* would, and that interpretation doesn't exist for (42). The suggested restriction about copied-in variables is untenable however, given the existence of sentences like (47), where *him* will be translated as a free variable and interpreted pragmatically with respect to the context. After the copying of the translation of the first VP into the second conjunct, we will have a copied-in free variable which is similarly assigned the same value as the first occurrence of the variable.

(47) Fred saw him and Peter did too.

What all this means then is that different occurrences of the same variable must be treated in the same way, i.e. all as bound variables or all as free variables assigned some value with respect to the context. So, in (46), the second occurrence of P_2 should be treated as the first occurrence, as a bound variable; but the second occurrence isn't bound, and since it may not be assigned some value with respect to the context, (46) will be excluded because it contains a variable which is neither bound nor assigned some value pragmatically. Mechanically, if we mark in a special way bound variables, we will ensure that P_2 in the second conjunct will be identified as a to-be-bound variable, and it will not be interpreted pragmatically.

We may conclude that representations like (45) must be preferred to representations like (43), and that questions like (40) may not be given a representation as in (iii) in (41).

How should (40) be represented then? One possible way would be to associate a performative operator with each conjunct, so that each conjunct would be an expression of category *t*. Another one would be to allow conjoining of expressions of different categories, acknowledging that there is something we generally don't understand about conjoining, since there are apparently other unexplained cases of conjoining of expressions belonging to different categories, as we will see. We will briefly examine each possibility.

2.2.2.2 A solution.

Assuming the presence of a performative operator with each conjunct, (42) would be represented as in (48):

(48) $[[?\lambda a^t[j*(a^t(\char94 leave'))]] \& [?\lambda P[j*(\char94 take (P))]]]$

Does such a representation lead to problems? I don't see any in this particular case, but it is certainly inappropriate for questions such as (49):

(49) Do you want tea or do you want coffee?

We will examine alternative questions later. Anticipating a little, it is clear that we don't want an interpretation that can be paraphrased by (50):

(50) I ask you to tell me whether you want tea or I ask you to tell me whether you want coffee.

But the problem that existed with (40) doesn't exist with (49): each member of the alternative question belongs to the same category, and so they can be conjoined directly.

Some problems may arise however with embedded conjoined wh-questions. Consider the following example:

(51) Who will marry who and when all these marriages are going to take place is going to be decided at the next meeting.

In (51), the first wh-clause is of category (t/T)/T and the second one of category t/IAV, and they shouldn't be able to be conjoined. Trying to derive (51) from (52) wouldn't help, if, as seems likely, the requirement that conjuncts be of the same category holds at all levels in a derivation:

(52) Who will marry who is going to be decided at the next meeting and when all these marriages are going to take place is going to be decided at the next meeting.

The problem with conjunction of questions may be taken as an indication that the approach we are exploring is misguided, or that there should be some rule which turns all questions into expressions of the same category, or that we don't understand how conjoining works. This last position is that taken, with respect to other sorts of problems, by Jackendoff (1977:190-194) for example. In the next section we will give some cases suggesting that the latter may very well be the case.

2.2.2.3 Coordination of expressions belonging to different categories.

Consider the following examples:

(53) a. It was by going through the files that I discovered what a big salary he had, how he got it, and whether he deserved it.

b. He knows what he is capable of and that he has not done it. (The Globe)

c. John learned that he was going to be fired and for what reasons.

(54) a. ...turning to the semantics and how to constrain it... (Partee, 1976:104)

b. How this process works and the reasons behind it will be clarified soon.

c. Shut the door and would you please turn on the lights?

In (53) we find complements which in Chomsky s framework would be analyzed as belonging to the syntactic category $\bar{S}$, and there is some dispute as to whether the indirect question is in addition dominated by NP while the that-complement is not (see Bresnan and Grimshaw, 1978). Semantically however we have different kinds of complements for sure: propositions, questions, exclamations. Just as one expects only expressions of the same category to be conjoined, it would seem that only expressions of the same semantic type would be conjoined. Turning to (54)a,b we find a wh-question and an NP (used as a concealed question) conjoined. Unless the wh-question is an NP, as argued by Bresnan and Grimshaw (1978), these would be examples of conjunction of expressions belonging to different syntactic categories, $\bar{S}$ and NP, in the standard framework of transformational grammar. In (54)c an imperative and a question are conjoined, but the question is to be taken as a command. In Montague's framework the expressions conjoined in (53) and (54) would be analyzed by most people as belonging to different categories. It seems that what is necessary for those cases then is some way to turn expressions belonging to certain different categories into expressions of the same category. If this is the way that such examples should be treated, it might be the way that we should treat conjoined wh-questions. Until we have a better understanding of how the grammar of conjunction works it is difficult to draw conclusions from questions such as (42) and (52) for the analysis of questions we are investigating.

2.2.3 Embedding of questions.

The problem here arises, as in the preceding section, from the fact that different questions may belong to different categories and types; in fact, Hausser's and Zaefferer's approach allows for infinitely many categories of questions, given the existence of iterative questions. This means that each verb that takes an indirect question has to be split into an infinite number of homophonous verbs of the appropriate categories. For example, assuming indirect questions to be identical to direct ones, which is not Hausser's position, as we will soon see, we already need three verbs *to know* for the three questions in (55), each of them being a member of the category indicated.

(55) a. John knows who came. [*know* = IV/(t/t/T)]

b. John knows why Peter came. [*know* = IV/(t/IAV)]

c. John knows who gave what to whom. [*know* = IV/(((t/T)/T)/T)]

Something similar, but in a minimal way, arises in Karttunen's analysis also, questions being of a different category, and thus of a different type, than propositions. Karttunen is however able to relate one verb to another by a meaning postulate, while it seems that here we would need some system to generate all those homophonous verbs from one of them.

Good evidence has been given by Grimshaw (1977, Chapter V) that each of these verbs that may take both a question or a proposition as complement should have only one lexical entry because they behave as one verb with respect to whether or not they may have a null complement: if a verb may take a null complement, and it may also take a question and a proposition as complement, then the null complement is interpretable as a question or as a proposition, depending on whether there is a question or a proposition in the linguistic context that can serve as controller for the null complement. The following examples illustrate this:

(56) a. Peter left. -I know.

b. Who left? -I don't know.

According to Grimshaw (1977:109) it is unlikely that one can predict which verbs have the property of taking null complements, and verbs have to be individually marked as to whether they may have a null complement, i.e., in her framework, verbs that allow null complements are simply subcategorized for an optional $\overline{S}$ complement. If there is only one entry for *know*, for example, it is expected that we will find the same behaviour with respect to the null complement whether we have the know-that or the know-wh verb. In Karttunen's theory,

where the two *know*'s are simply related by a meaning postulate, the
similar behaviour is not predicted, and this becomes a problem when
we see that it repeats itself for many verbs. In the analysis we
are exploring, things would be even worse, unless *know* and other
similar verbs are treated as verbs of FLOATING TYPE, following
Parsons (1977). With T standing for an arbitrary type, *know* can be
assigned to category (type) IV/T. Here T must in fact range over
t for propositional complements and over all the types of questions.
Some way must be found to restrict the range of T. I will assume
it can be done and that Parsons' idea of floating type is what is
needed here (or in Karttunen's analysis). Another possibility, which
would carry over to the conjunction problem, would be to have a meaning postulate turning all questions into a unique type; but since
this type couldn't be t, it seems, the floating type solution, but
more restricted, would still be needed.

2.2.4 Extensional and intensional interpretation.

One of the arguments given by Hausser and Zaefferer (1976:12-14)
as support for their analysis is that they can account for the ambiguity of question-answer pairs like (57)a, which has the same readings
as (57)b.

(57) a. What does Mary imagine? A dragon.

b. Mary imagines a dragon.

Montague accounts for the non-referential, or intensional, reading
of (57)b by constructing the VP (the IV) by putting the verb *imagine*
and the object *a dragon* immediately together, and he accounts for
the referential or extensional reading by quantifying in *a dragon*$_o$
into *Mary imagines he*$_o$. The meanings corresponding to the two derivations are different. Hausser and Zaefferer try to reproduce the
same analysis for the question-answer pair (57)a. One important
feature of their analysis is that they treat the question part of
(57)a as unambiguous but the question-answer pair as ambiguous.
We will come back to this later, but first see how their account
works. Letting $^\vee P$ translate *what*, the question is translated as
(58):

(58) $\lambda Pm*(^\wedge \text{imagine}'(P))$

That is, *what* itself is given narrow scope, it is not quantified
in. To get the non-referential reading of the question-answer pair,
they simply let the context-variable Γ take as argument the intensional-
ized translation of *a dragon*, as in (59)a; the context-variable is
then replaced by the translation of the question, as in (59)b, which
is equivalent to (59)d, the desired reading:

(59) a. Γ (P̂ Vx[dragon'(x) & P{x}])

   b. λPm*(^imagine'(P))(P̂ Vx[dragon'(x) & P{x}])

   c. m*(^imagine'(P̂ Vx[dragon'(x) & P{x}])).

   d. imagine' (^m,P̂ Vx[dragon'(x) & P{x}])

The referential reading is obtained, as for (57)b, by quantifying in the translation of a *dragon* into (60)a, i.e. the non-redundant answer is translated as in (60)b:

(60) a. Γ(P̂ P{x_n})

   b. P̂ Vx(dragon'(x) & P{x}](x̂_n Γ(PP{x_n}))

Replacing Γ by the translation of the question, we obtain (61)a, which is equivalent to (61)b, whose interpretation is that of the referential reading.

(61) a. P̂ Vx[dragon'(x) & P{x}](x̂_n [λPm*(^imagine'(P))])
          (ᵖP{x_n}))

   b. Vu[dragon'_*(u) & imagine'_*(m,u)]

Mechanically there is nothing wrong with this, but not considering the question as ambiguous is incorrect. First the ambiguity arises in indirect questions as well, and there, there is no answer to get one or the other of the readings:

(62) I wonder what Mary is looking for.

And depending on the wh-phrase and our knowledge of the world, the referential or non-referential reading is more likely to arise:

(63) a. I wonder what book Mary is looking for.

   b. I wonder what new enemy Don Quixote is looking for.

In addition, in languages like French there are syntactic reflexes of each reading if the direct object contains a relative clause: with the indicative we have the referential reading, with the subjunctive the non-referential one.

(64) a. Marie cherche une robe qui lui aille bien.

         Mary is looking for a dress that would suit her well.

   b. Que cherches-tu qui t'aille bien?

         What are you looking for that would suit you well?

(65) a. Marie cherche une robe qui lui va bien.
Mary is looking for a dress that suits her well.

b. Que cherches-tu qui te va bien?
What are you looking for that suits you well?

It is possible to account for each type of interpretation by quantifying in the wh-phrase for the referential reading, and by generating it in place for the non-referential reading, just as in the case of the assertion.

The non-referential reading would be obtained by translation (58), with the '?' operator added in front. There, the relation *imagine'* holds between Mary and some properties of properties of individual concepts. The referential reading is obtained through a translation such as in (66)a, which is equivalent to (66)b:

(66) a. $?\lambda P^v P\{\hat{x}[m*(imagine'(\hat{P}P\{x\}))])$

b. $?\lambda P^v P(\hat{u}[imagine'_*(m,u)])$

Here the relation *imagine'* holds between Mary and an individual.

The non-redundant answer to both (58) and (66) is (59)a. When the context-variable is replaced by (58), we derive (59)d. When it is replaced by (66), we derive (61)b. The question however is whether wh-phrases can be generated in place, i.e. not quantified in. Facts with VP-interpretation show that some binding takes place: with ordinary quantifiers this would be evidence for quantifying in. Here however, the analysis with λ binding a variable makes it impossible to be sure whether the wh-phrase must be quantified in.

2.2.5. <u>Surface non-redundant answers</u>.

We have seen that the wh-PHRASE in questions was of the type of the intension of the minimal answer. The variable that is abstracted upon is not necessarily of the intension of the type of the wh-WORD itself. So, while the variable involved when the wh-word was *who* was of the type of the intension of *who*, i.e., $<s,<<s, \ll s,e>,t>>,t>>$, the same variable is used with *which man*, but *which* is of the type $<<s,<<s,e>,t>>,<<s,<<s,e>,t>>t>>$. This is so because both (67)a and b take an NP as minimal answer:

(67) a. Who came?

b. Which person came?

One may however suggest that in (67)b, a minimal answer ought to be an expression of the type of the intension of the type of *which*, i.e. that the variable necessary to translate (67)b should be of that type. An answer like (68) would be considered as a partially redundant answer. It would be a property of the surface structure of English, i.e. what ellipses are possible, that would prevent a minimal, non-redundant answer in the case of questions like (67)b. One could even go further and say that in the case of (67)a too a full NP as an answer is redundant, since *who* is semantically analagous to *which person*. That sometimes partially redundant answers are imposed because of some syntactic restrictions is obvious, for example in the case of question-answer pairs like (68) in French:

(68) a. A qui as-tu parlé?
To whom did you speak?

b. A Pierre.
To Peter.

c. *Pierre.
Peter.

It seems that the restriction is related to the fact that dangling prepositions are not allowed in French, i.e. the preposition and its complement may not be separated. If there is some doubt as to whether (68)b is partially redundant, there is none with (69):

(69) a. Avec la soeur de qui Pierre est-il sorti?
With whose sister did Peter go out?

b. Avec celle de John.
With John's.

c. *?De John.
John's.

This shows that looking at actual question-answer pairs may suggest an analysis, but that the details of the analysis, e.g. what variable should be abstracted on, shouldn't come simply from the observation of what minimal answers a particular language allows. More sophisticated arguments should be used to justify a particular choice of variables. For example, if we wish to maintain that questions and free relatives should be analyzed in an identical way as far as the wh-clause is concerned, then we need variables of type $<s,e>$ if we want to translate a free relative such as (12)b by (12)c. I don't think it is possible to arrive at a satisfactory translation with the use of P. We may then try to show that variables of the type $<s,e>$ should be used in the parallel sorts of questions. More work is needed here to justify the decisions that have been made. I'll leave this for another time.

2.2.6 <u>Yes-no and alternative questions</u>.

Egli (1973), Hausser and Zaefferer (1976), and Hausser (1978) have the same approach to yes-no questions. We draw mainly here from Hausser and Zaefferer.

The minimal answers to yes-no questions are *yes* and *no*:

(70) a. Did John come?

   b. Yes.

   c. No.

We need suitable translations for *yes* and *no* and for the question so that they can fit together to give an expression of category and type t. They assume that q is a variable of type <s,f(t//t)> and we may then translate *whether* as $^{\vee}q$. *Yes* and *no* are translated as $\hat{p}[^{\vee}p]$ and $\hat{p}[-^{\vee}p]$ respectively. *Whether*, *yes*, and *no* are of category t//t and of type <<s,t>,t>. Syntactically, they derive direct yes-no questions like (70)a from something like (71), assuming some rule which gets rid of *whether*. Since I am not dealing with the syntax here, I refer the reader to their work for this aspect. (70)a-b can be translated as in (72):

(71) whether John did come.

(72) a. $?\lambda q[^{\vee}q(^{\wedge}came_{*}^{!}(j))]$

   $\Gamma(\hat{p}[^{\vee}p])$

Replacing Γ in (72)b by the lambda-expression of (72)a, we get (73)a, which is equivalent to (73)b. An answer like *yes* to (70)a is thus equivalent to an answer by a full proposition like (74).

(73) a. $\lambda q[^{\vee}q(^{\wedge}came_{*}^{!}(j))](\hat{p}[^{\wedge}p])$

   b. $came_{*}^{!}(j)$

(74) John came.

The problem comes in with alternative questions and with the desire that one may have to treat yes-no questions as similar semantically to alternative questions.

Egli is the only one to propose an analysis of alternative questions. Along his lines, (75) could be translated as (76) (ignoring tense):

(75) Did Peter come or did Fred come?

(76) $?\lambda q_1 \lambda q_2 \ [^{v}q_1(^{\wedge}\text{come}^!_*(p) \ \& \ q_2(^{\wedge}\text{come}^!_*(f)]$

That is, alternative questions are treated as a conjunction of yes-no questions. Another more common approach in DETAILED analysis of questions is to treat yes-no questions as reduced alternative questions or as equivalent to such questions; see Bolinger (1977) for references and, in my opinion, a misguided criticism of that approach.

The first problem that may arise with (76) is whether the lambda may be given scope over the two sentences. What we have seen in 2.2.2 with respect to coordination may suggest that it may not. It is however possible that things would be different here, since the bound variables are not within each sentence. The distribution of *whether* itself isn't an indication, if *whether* is simply translated as the variable that is abstracted on: so we have both (77)a and b:

(77) a. I wonder whether Peter will leave or whether Fred will.

b. I wonder whether Peter will leave or Fred will.

Another problem is the justification of the rendition of *or* by &. There are cases where it is clear that *or* seems to stand for &, as in the following example, from Ehrenkranz (1973):

(78) John is fatter than Fred or Paul.

One reading of (78) can be paraphrased by (79):

(79) John is fatter than Fred and John is fatter than Paul.

Thus it wouldn't be impossible for *or* in (75) to be translated by &. Intuitively, however, the *or* in (75) seems to be exclusive. This militates against translating *or* by & in (76). More work on *or* is however necessary before we can take a definitive stand on this problem. Notice that the first problem mentioned disappears if we translate (75) by (80):

(80) $?\lambda q_1 [^{v}q_1(^{\wedge}\text{come}^!_*(p))] \ \& \ ?\lambda q_2[^{v}q_2(^{\wedge}\text{come}^!_*(f))]$

But given (80) we would expect minimal answers like (81) to (75), but those are totally impossible:

(81) *yes no.

If we insist on the surface minimal answers to determine the correct analysis, the impossibility of (81) would go against analyses such as (76) or (80). Moreover, if one insists on relating yes-no questions to alternative ones, which is not unreasonable, given for example the fact that historically *whether* meant *which of two* (Jespersen, MEG, II:7.74) and that in many languages yes-no questions are marked by a morpheme similar to the morpheme for disjunction, then the analysis suggested for (70)a in (72)a might have to be replaced by something similar to (76) or (80), and such an analysis would predict answers like (81). I don't think that the surface answers to alternative and yes-no questions are a good indicator of how they should be analyzed, when we notice the variety of means that are used to answer them in different languages.

The traditional view in detailed studies of questions, which takes alternative questions as basic, and yes-no questions as a special case of alternative questions, seems intuitively more satisfying. An alternative question offers a set of propositions, and one of them is presupposed true. So an answer is one of the propositions. A yes-no question also offers an alternative, but between two propositions, one of which is the negation of the other. An answer is one of them. An answer such as *yes* or *no* may be taken as shorthand for a full answer. Since only one of the propositions is given on the surface, saying *yes* is agreeing to that proposition, saying *no* is rejecting it and thus taking the other unexpressed proposition as true. Slight support for that may be found in the fact that it is quite normal to give after *yes* or *no* the proposition that is taken as true.

(82) a. Did Peter leave?

b. Yes, he did/he left.

c. No, he didn't (leave).

If alternative questions are taken as basic then it would seem that the analysis proposed by Karttunen (1977a) is the more appropriate. (82)a would translate as (83) and (75) as (84):

(83) $\lambda p[^{\vee}p \ \& \ [p=\,^{\wedge}\text{leave}'_{*}(p) \ \vee \ p=\,^{\wedge}-\text{leave}'_{*}(j)]]$

(84) $\lambda p[^{\vee}p \ \& \ [p=\,^{\wedge}\text{come}'_{*}(p) \ \vee \ p=\,^{\wedge}\text{come}'_{*}(f)]]$

If Karttunen's approach must be taken for these questions, then we would have two sorts of semantics of questions, one for wh-questions, another one for yes-no and alternative questions. This would appear as a weakness in the analysis, especially when there is an alternative analysis that has a uniform treatment for all questions. At this time, alternative questions thus seem the weakest spot in the analysis discussed.

2.2.7 Ungrammatical yes-no questions.

2.2.7.1

The ungrammaticality of sentences like (85) is well-known, and several proposals have been made in order to account for that; see for example Baker (1968:60sqq), Wachowicz (1974:96-98), Nakada (1976: 56-58), Karttunen (1977a:21-23, 25-26) and Hausser (1978:230-236).

(85) *John wonders whether who came.

Baker (1968:60) stated the facts as follows:

> It seems in general to be the case that the disjuncts in a *whether* question may not themselves be questions.

And he proposes the following constraint:

> If S is one disjunct in a whether-question, then S must not have associated with it any occurence of a wh.

Another way to put this would be to say that another wh-word may not have scope over the same sentence as *whether* has.

Since Bakers', some proposals have been made from which this constraint would simply follow. The one most often suggested is examined below.

2.2.7.2

We will begin by examining Hausser's theory, which is similar to that proposed by Nakada and Wachowicz. This will give us the opportunity to show that embedded questions shouldn't be analyzed as open formulae as Hausser proposes.

Hausser (1976:231) considers "*whether* as an operator of category t//t which takes a closed sentence as argument and results in an OPEN sentence". In addition, while he takes direct questions to be abstracts, he analyzes indirect questions as open sentential complements, as open formulae. So, (86)a is translated as (86)b and (87)a as (87)b.

(86) a. Did John come?

b. $\lambda q^{\vee} q(^\wedge come_*^!(j))$

(87) a. Peter wonders whether John came.

b. $p*(^\wedge wonders'(q(^\wedge come_*^!(j))))$

The ungrammaticality of (85) is then apparently easy to explain. *Who came* in (85) will be analyzed as an open formula, and it should combine with *whether*, but it cannot because *whether* takes only a closed sentence as argument. The same holds for direct questions such as (88)a, which Hausser derives from (88)b:

(88) a. *Did who come?

b. Whether who came.

(85) and (88)a are translated by (89)a and b respectively, taking $^{\vee}P$ to be a sorted variable for *who*.

(89) a. $j*(^\wedge wonder'(q(P(^\wedge come'))$

b. $\lambda q^{\vee} q(P(^\wedge come'))$

Let us quote Hausser (pp. 235-236):

> The central issue of yes/no questions is *truth*. Yes/no questions inquire whether a certain sentence is to be taken to be true or false.... In order to be able to determine the truth of an expression ϕ, however, two requirements have to be fulfilled: ϕ has to be of type t, and ϕ may not contain any unbound variables. It is the second condition which rules out the presence of any questioned elements in ϕ, if ϕ is to function as a constituent in a yes/no question.... This explains why direct as well as indirect yes/no questions are necessarily unary.

The same idea is found in Wachowicz (1974:97-98), who gives credit to Stanley Peters.

> A sentence containing a wh-word, which is a free variable, is comparable to an open formula in logic. One cannot assign a truth value to an open formula without first assigning an interpretation to the free variable. Thus, there is a semantic order in asking questions: first assign an interpretation to all the free variables, that is to wh-words in the sentence, and then ask about the truth value of the sentence, i.e. ask a 'yes-no' question.

But in fact, as first pointed out to me by Barbara Hall Partee, the requirement that the argument of *whether* be a closed sentence is too strong, in view of sentences like (90)a, translated as (90)b, in this system:

(90) a. Some man wonders whether he is a fool.

b. Vx [man(x) & wonder'(x, q(^fool'(x))]

Here the argument of q, which translates ^*whether*', is an open formula. The difference with (89)a for example is that here the variable is bound from OUTSIDE. In doing the evaluation of the whole sentence, given the semantics of *some*, arbitrary assignments of values to the variable x will be made, and this is what matters.

More interesting is the case of sentences like (91):

(91) John told Fred which book he wondered whether he should read.

Remember that in Hausser's system, the wh-words are generated in place: (91) will then be translated as (92):

(92) j*($\hat{x}_1$[λPP{x_1}(^tell'($\hat{P}$P{^f},^($\hat{P}$P{x_1}(^wonder'(q

($\hat{P}$P{x_1}(^should'(^read'($\hat{P}^v$P($\hat{z}$[book'(z) & P{z}])))))))])

If we accept every bit of Hausser's analysis, the argument of *whether* (i.e. of ˇq) is an open formula with the free variable corresponding to the wh-word not even bound from outside. This shows at least one of two things: the variable should be bound from outside in the way it was in direct questions, i.e. by the lambda that is used to make questions, or the wh-phrase must be quantified in at the right moment, so that the argument of *whether*' will contain only variables bound from outside. If we take the second tack, (91) will be translated by (93):

(93) j*($\hat{x}_1$[λPP{x_1}(^tell'($\hat{P}$P{^f} ($\hat{P}^v$P($\hat{z}$[book'(z) & P{z}])

($\hat{y}$[$\hat{P}$P{x_1}(^wonder'(q($\hat{P}$P{x_1}(^should'(^read'($\hat{P}$P{y})))))

])))])

That some binding is at work can independently be seen by using the VP-deletion test again. So (94) is ungrammatical:

(94) *John wonders which boy touched which car and which girl did too.

We have seen in 2.2.2 that the ungrammaticality resulted from the fact that in the translation, there was a free variable corresponding to *which car* (and this free variable couldn't be interpreted pragmatically because it had to be interpreted in the same way as a previous occurrence of the same variable, which was bound). If we adopt Hausser's analysis of indirect questions, nothing will distinguish the translation of the VP in the first conjunct from the translation of the VP in the second conjunct. Quantifying in the wh-phrases or having the variable of the wh-phrase bound by lambda as in direct questions will give the means to account for (94) and (91).

Remember now how we suggested that the question in (57)a, repeated here as (95), could be accounted for:

(95) What does Mary imagine?

We took advantage of the possibility of quantifying in *what* or generating it immediately as the complement of *imagine* and of having to bind the free variable that was part of the translation of the wh-phrase by λ. If this is the correct way to account for the ambiguity of (95), then the ambiguity of (96)a should be accounted for in the same way, i.e., we would need both quantifying in of wh-phrase (for the referential reading) and binding of the variable that is part of the translation of the wh-phrase by lambda (for the non-referential reading) since (96)b, where the VP in the second conjunct is absent, is ungrammatical, whatever the reading that one tries to impose on the first conjunct.

(96) a. John wonders what Mary imagines.

  b. *John wonders [what Mary imagines and what Peter does too.]

We can then come back to the problem we started with, the ungrammaticality of sentences like (85) and (88)a. It is clear why they are ungrammatical if we assume a derivation where we try to put together *whether* and a wh-question: *whether* must take an expression of type t as argument, i.e. a sentence, open or not; but a wh-question as analyzed here, is never of type t, it is not an expression that can have a truth-value as denotation (so, the intuition that many people have had is simply implemented in another way). This account is the same as that given by Karttunen, the only difference being in the particular translation given for questions, which is irrelevant here. One problem remains however. We don't have a way to exclude the derivation of (97)a that would be obtained by quantifying in who_n into (97)b:

(97) a. whether who came

b. whether he$_n$ came

The resulting translation is given in (98)a, equivalent to (98)b:

(98) a. $\lambda q_2 \lambda P^\vee P(\hat{x}[\lambda q_1[^\vee q_1(\hat{P}P\{x\}(^\wedge come'))]])$

b. $\lambda q_2 \lambda P^\vee P(\hat{x}[^\vee q_2(\hat{P}P\{x\}(^\wedge come'))])$

(98) is a multiple question. Anticipating what we will say about multiple questions, I think that (99)a,b,c would be appropriate answers:

(99) a. Yes Peter, no Mary.

b. Yes Peter, Anna, and Sue; no Bill, Fred, and Joyce.

c. Yes Peter, Anna, etc.; no Bill, Fred, etc.

That is, one can tentatively assign *yes* for *q*, and then a value for P. Or one can tentatively assign *no* and then one has to assign a value for P such that when the result is combined with *no* we have a true sentence.

Giving *yes* as a TENTATIVE value for q results in (100), which has to be answered appropriately; taking then *no* gives (101), which also has to be answered appropriately:

(100) a. $\lambda q_2 \lambda P^\vee P(\hat{x}[^\vee q_2(^\wedge come'(x))])(\hat{p}[^\vee p])$

b. $\lambda P^\vee P(\hat{x}[\hat{p}[^\vee p](^\wedge come'(x))])$

c. $\lambda P^\vee P(\hat{x}[come'(x)])$

(101) a. $\lambda q_2 \lambda P^\vee P(\hat{x}[^\vee q_2(^\wedge come'(x))])(\hat{p}[-^\vee p])$

b. $\lambda P^\vee P(\hat{x}[\hat{p}[-^\vee p](^\wedge come'(x))])$

c. $\lambda P^\vee P(\hat{x}[-come'(x)])$

We obtain the same sort of result if we allow quantification of *who* into a whether-clause in Karttunen's system (Karttunen doesn't allow it; we will come to this in a moment); in his system the translation for (97)a would be (see Karttunen, 1977:21-22):

(102) a. p̂ [Vx [ᵛp & [p=ˆcome!₊(ᵛx) v p=ˆ-come!₊(ᵛx)]]]

(102) denotes the set containing all true propositions expressed by sentences of the form 'x came' and 'x didn't come', i.e. it denotes a set which contains, for each person who came, the proposition that he came, and for each person who didn't come, the proposition that he didn't come. That is, under this derivation, (85), repeated here, would be taken to be equivalent to (103):

(85) *John wonders whether who came.

(103) John wonders for every person whether that person came (or not).

(103) is good. A direct question like (88) would then have to be answered by a list of the people who came and a list of the people who didn't come. How does Karttunen prevent quantifying in wh-phrases into whether-questions? Simply by saying that this is not allowed, i.e. by writing the rule for wh-quantification so that this is impossible. Some historical background on how this "constraint" developed may be useful.

Originally (1975), Karttunen derived questions like (104)a by quantifying in who' into (104)b, which was then translated as (104)c.

(104) a. Who came?

b. whether he$_n$ came

c. p̂[ᵛp & p=ˆφ']

The quantification rule simply substituted who for whether and the translation was as in (105):

(105) p̂ Vx [ᵛp & p=ˆcome!₊(ᵛx)]

The rule of wh-quantification was however such that it could not quantify into an alternative question, because the translation would have been as in (106) for (104)a, which is obviously the wrong meaning:

(106) p̂ Vx [ᵛp & [p=ˆcome!₊(ᵛx) v p=ˆ-come!₊(ᵛx)]]

In (1977a,b) yes-no questions are translated as alternative questions so that the derivation of questions like (104)a from (104)b, which no longer translated as (104)c, had to be blocked. But once we accept that questions like (104)a should not be derived from yes-no questions, the fact that (85) is out is explained only by brute force, i.e. simply by saying that quantifying in a wh-phrase into a whether-clause is not allowed.

2.3 Conclusion

Exploring the consequences of analyzing questions along the lines of Egli (1973,1974), Hull (1974,1975), Hull and Keenan (1973a,1973b), Hausser and Zaefferer (1976) and Hausser (1978), in the framework of Hausser and Zaefferer (1976) and Hausser (1978), the main points we have made are that:

1) it is necessary to derive direct questions from indirect questions in order to account for some scope ambiguities (see 2.2.1)

2) there remain difficulties with coordination (2.2.2) and embedding (2.2.3) of questions, difficulties which may not be that important in fact

3) the analyses of alternative questions that we have considered are still unattractive and more work is needed here. I refer the reader to recent work by Hausser (to appear, section 5) that I haven't had the time to study and report here for another account of alternative questions

4) indirect questions should not be treated as open formulae.

Some suggestions have also been made that would account for the ungrammaticality of questions like (85).

(85) *John wonders whether who came.

In the next chapter we will examine multiple questions and see that they may provide evidence for the approach to questions considered in Chapter II.

CHAPTER III

MULTIPLE QUESTIONS

3.0 Introduction

In this chapter we will see how the analysis discussed accounts for the sorts of answers that can be given to multiple questions, especially to those where the wh-phrases are in the singular, as in (1):

(1) Which boy kissed which girl?

Before doing this, we will discuss what sorts of answers can be given to multiple questions, i.e. we will examine whether or not it is the case, as claimed by Wachowicz (1974), that a direct answer to a multiple question must be a conjunction of sentences (what we will call a multiple answer) rather than a single one.

3.1. Answers to multiple questions

In *On the Syntax and the Semantics of Multiple Questions*, Wachowicz claims that in ORDINARY DISCOURSE (which excludes echo and quiz questions), a multiple question requires a multiple answer. So, while (3) would be a possible answer to (2), (4) would not:

(2) Who is leaving when?

(3) Herbert is leaving in May and Monica in December.

(4) Herbert is leaving in May.

The same claim can be found in Kuno and Robinson (1972:432-3), who insist that sentences like (4) are felt as incomplete answers to questions like (2). Hankamer makes an observation of the same sort with respect to the multiple questions he discusses (1975:73, fn.3), without implying that this would be general for all sorts of multiple questions.

Wachowicz also claims that ordinary multiple questions are "requests for information on how to pair up the elements for which wh-words stand, rather than requests for identity " (1974:26). Later she adds that "in multiple questions each of the wh-words stands for at least two members" (p. 29). Here *to stand for* means *to be in the place of the appropriate values*; we will use the term in the same way.[1]

From this it follows, according to her (p. 26), that the answer to a multiple question must be a multiple answer, but she doesn't say how it follows.

I will support the view that both of Wachowicz's claims are incorrect, i.e. multiple questions can be used as requests for identification of appropriate values (in addition, when there is more than one pair or triple, etc. it is obvious that for the answer to be true we need appropriate pairings), and multiple questions don't necessarily have to be answered by multiple answers.

We may start by considering the four sorts of answers that a question such as (2), repeated here, may try to elicit:

(2) Who is leaving when?

There are four cases with respect to whether or not the person who asks (2) knows what is going to be substituted for the wh-words in the answer.

   a) The speaker knows who the persons who left are, and at what times there were departures, but he doesn't know the appropriate pairings.[2]

   b) He only knows who the persons who left are.

   c) He only knows the times of departures.

   d) He neither knows who left nor what the departure times were.

We may eliminate the second situation, since, when what one wh-phrase stands for is known while what the other stands for is not, it is the latter which moves in Comp.[3]

Consider the first situation. If at least one of the wh-words will be replaced in the answer by only one value, for example *yesterday* for *when*, there is no justification for using *when* instead of *yesterday*: using *when* would be misleading since it would be taken as indicating that the pairing is not known. For the pairings not to be known when the values for *who* and *when* are known is possible only when *who* will take more than one value and when *when* will do the same. A question like (2) in the first situation can thus elicit only multiple answers. This has however nothing to do with the semantics of the multiple question itself.

The same can be said about the third situation. If the speaker knows that *when* takes only one value and knows that value, the wh-word shouldn't be used. Also, if *when* stands for several values that

are known but the only thing that is known about *who* is that it
will take one value, then *when* shouldn't be used either, but rather
a question like (5), if *tomorrow*, *Monday*, and *Saturday* are the relevant
days:

(5) Who is leaving tomorrow, again on Monday, and again on
Saturday?

Using (2) would be taken as implying that the necessary information
to ask (5) was not present, so there must have been at least two
individuals, and so we can only expect multiple answers in the third
case.

In the fourth situation we may expect either a single or a
multiple answer. Wachowicz expresses doubts however as to whether a
question like (2) can be used at all when the values for neither of
the wh-phrases are known to the questioner. We will see that (2)
can be used in these circumstances and in particular when there is
only one pair. Before coming to that we will consider some examples
that Wachowicz gives as support for her claim that multiple questions
always need multiple answers. Her claim predicts that questions
where it is not possible that the wh-phrase stands for more than one
value will be ungrammatical (except if an 'echo' or 'quiz' question
interpretation is given). The following examples, if the judgments
are correct, support her position:

(6) a. *Who killed Robert Kennedy when?

b. *Who is keeping the silver dollar in which bank?

c. *Who put my car through which car shredder?

In the absence of appropriate contexts suggested to them, informants tend to go along with these judgments. But consider the first
example with the following situation. Some journalist has two suspects
in mind, Peter and Bill, and in fact he knows that either Peter killed
Kennedy at 8:35 p.m. or that Bill killed him at 8:35 and 12 seconds.
If he can become sure of the time of the murder he will know who the
murderer was, and conversely. Some dependency is thus created between
murderer and time. In such a context, informants find (6)a much better.
Similarly with (6)c: suppose your insurance company is going to pay
you only if you can establish who put your car in some car shredder
and which car shredder your car was pushed through, then, it is easy
to imagine yourself going around asking (6)c, waiting for an answer
like:

(7) Big Joe put your car through car shredder 2.

We will see other clearer examples later.

One thing which seems to play a role here is that there is an alternative way to ask these questions, for example:

(8) a. Who killed Robert Kennedy, and when?

b. Who is keeping the silver dollar, and in which bank?

c. Who put my car through some car shredder, and through which?

The difference between (6) and (8), I think, comes from one aspect of multiple question: somehow, it seems that the value for one of the wh-phrases depends on the value for the other. This is clear in cases involving several pairs, as in (2)-(3): if you start with *Herbert* you have to take *May* because of that choice, and if you had started with *Monica* you would have had to take *December* because of that choice too. Similarly with (6)a: in the context we gave, answering with *Peter* would force you to take 8 35 p.m. as the time. However, in the absence of the information about the relation between murderer and time, the answer to one variable doesn't provide the answer to the other one. A question like (8)a makes this absence of dependency clear, and it may be preferred perhaps for that reason. We will see other examples however where no dependency between the value for each wh-phrase exists, but where a multiple question is however perfect.

The first sort of example comes from Wachowicz herself (1974:29), who cites Aqvist. According to Aqvist, (9)b is an appropriate answer to (9)a. Wachowicz claims that this is not true in ordinary language.

(9) a. What maestro is conducting what orchestra in the performance of what symphony at tonight's concert?

b. Bernstein is conducting the Boston Symphony Orchestra in the performance of Beethoven's Fifth Symphony at tonight's concert.

Wachowicz says that in normal conversation, (9)a would be pronounced with an intonation break after every question phrase, which indicates, according to her, that it comes from a CONJUNCTION [my emphasis] and is a request for identity rather than a request for pairing. Wachowicz also claims that (9)a is not a normal request for identity and assimilates it to a quiz question, rather.

First of all, besides an answer like (9)b, (9)a could have (10) as an appropriate answer, in cases where two different maestros conduct two different orchestras in the performance of two different symphonies at the same concert.

(10) Bernstein is conducting the Boston Symphony Orchestra in the performance of Beethoven's Fifth Symphony and Solti is conducting the Chicago Symphony Orchestra in the performance of Mahler's Ninth Symphony at tonight's concert.

(10) would then be an answer to (9)a understood as a genuine multiple question: it is unlikely that (9)b would be an answer to (9)a with a certain intonation and that (10) would be an answer to (9)a with another intonation. In addition, all the speakers I have asked agree that (9)a would be totally natural in the context of a music festival, where each evening a different orchestra plays under the direction of a guest conductor, if the speaker doesn't know the program. It would be equivalent to asking (11):

(11) What is the program tonight?

Wachowicz contrasts (9)a with (12), a reduced version of it, and points out that (12) has what she considers the normal interpretation, i.e. it elicits normally an answer made of a set of propositions:

(12) What maestro is conducting what orchestra?

And she uses that contrast to say that (9)a is special. There is however nothing strange here: (12) is simply a very general question about all the conductors who conduct some orchestra. As soon as some additional restrictive specification is added, a non-multiple answer is again quite perfect, for example, in the context of a music festival.

(13) What maestro is conducting what orchestra at tonight's concert?

Two other similar examples are discussed by Wachowicz (p. 30), who claims they are examination questions:

(14) a. What princess ran away with what prince, according to what fairy tale?

b. What French Emperor defeated what Russian Tsar in the last century?

Hull (1974) disagrees with Wachowicz's intuitions that such questions are necessarily examination questions: they are "much easier to imagine used in puzzle or exam situations than as genuine requests for information" (p. 265), but they can be used as genuine requests for information provided the appropriate context. I refer the reader to Hull's discussion (p. 265).

Other counter-examples are found in Kuno and Robinson (1972). They involve indirect questions. The most striking one is (15):

(15) Which one of you kids is going to tell me who stole this candy bar from where?

John probably is -- the dirty rat fink!

The answer can be seen as a shortened form of (16):

(16) John probably is going to tell you who stole this candy bar from where.

The most likely interpretation of the embedded question is that one individual is involved in the stealing and that it took place in only one place. (15) and (16) are however perfect sentences.

The two other examples in Kuno and Robinson are (17)a and (17)b:

(17) a. Who asked you when Columbus discovered what?

b. Who remembers who discovered what on October 12, 1492?

It may happen that some people collapse Columbus' several voyages of discovery to a single event, i.e. the "discovery of America". For those people, the embedded sentence in (17)a is understood as involving only one pair (Columbus discovered America on October 12, 1492), and the same is possible for (17)b. (17)b can easily be considered as a quiz question; this is less likely for (17)a and totally out for (15). None of them is to be taken as a quiz question.

One impression I have is that multiple questions involving only one pair are easier to accept as embedded questions than as direct questions:

(18) a. Who killed Hoffa when, that is what the police have been trying to find out during the last two years.

b. Unless I find out who put my car through which car shredder the insurance company won't reimburse me.

c. The discussions about who is keeping the silver dollar in which bank are quite boring.

Why this is so is unclear to me.

The second class of counter-examples (or apparent counter-examples) discussed by Wachowicz is well-known: it involves what she calls reciprocal verbs, but a better name would be REVERSIBLE VERBS or verbs with reversible arguments, as in (19):

(19) Who hit who (first)?

(20) is a perfect answer to it, for example when it is known that two people are involved:

(20) Peter hit Fred (first).

Wachowicz proposes to give (19) a semantic representation as in (21):

(21) Either A hit B or B hit A.

For Wachowicz, single answers are natural only with reversible verbs.

Let us notice first that deriving multiple questions from real disjunctions would be impossible in the case where we would have an infinite disjunction, as would be the case for examples like (22):

(22) Which real number is a multiple of which other real number?

Notice by the way that it is just as plausible to derive single wh-questions from disjunctions as it is for multiple questions (or just as implausible). For example, in a world with three individuals besides Peter, (23) could be represented, in Wachowicz's spirit, as in (24):

(23) Who killed Peter?

(24) Either A killed Peter or B killed Peter or C killed Peter.

We have considered (19) with a context where only two people were involved. There are similar examples, like (25), where the answer must be chosen from a large number of possibilities, and only a non-multiple answer is possible:

(25) I wonder which team is going to meet which (other) team in the next final of the World Soccer Cup.

An infinite number of such examples can be constructed. At the moment I see no reason to consider multiple questions as different in nature from non-multiple ones, and the same sort of analysis should therefore be given. Some multiple questions, such as those in (6), are odd for many speakers until an appropriate context is provided. I have no explanation for this. In the next section we will see how the analysis considered thus far can account for some multiple questions which at the moment are a problem for Karttunen.

3.2 Towards an analysis of multiple questions

Consider (26)a and (26)b:

(26) a. Which boy likes Mary?

b. Which boys like Mary?

(26)a is a request for an answer like (27)a, and (26)b for one like (27)b.

(27) a. Peter likes Mary.

b. Peter and Fred like Mary.

Consider (28) now:

(28) Which boy likes which girl?

There are two sorts of answers that (28) can elicit: a multiple one and a non-multiple one, depending on what the facts are and each time one person is paired with only one other person.

(29) a. Fred likes Sue and Harry likes Amanda.

b. Fred likes Sue.

This is a problem for Karttunen, who, as we will see, predicts the existence of answers like (29)b only: "...the set denoted by this instantiation question should contain only one proposition, say, that John likes Mary" (Karttunen, 1977b:22). He is however not sure that this is the correct result. Earlier (p. 14), he says: "In spite of the singularity of the wh-phrases, I am not sure that the question implicates that there ought to be a one-sentence answer, such as 'Mary likes John', although this is what my analysis predicts. If there is any uniqueness implicature at all, it perhaps has to do with each girl being paired with at most one boy, and vice versa, but I am not sure about this." Outside of any context, the most natural answer to a question like (28), for all speakers I have asked, and it is the same for me with the parallel French examples, is one involving several pairings, i.e. a multiple answer. The only problem is whether there is any uniqueness implicature. Some interesting observations on this problem have been made by Wachowicz. She claims that in (30), we have "a function from girls to errors which assigns to each girl one error. Another way of putting this is to say that (30) presupposes that each girl who noticed an error noticed only one, but the same error may have been noticed by more than one girl" (Wachowicz, 1974:41).

(30) Tell me which error was noticed by which girl.

And she claims that in (31) for each error only one girl noticed it, but a girl may have noticed more than one error. This amounts to claiming that we have a function from values for the unmoved wh-word to the values for the moved one.

(31) Tell me which girl noticed which error.

My own judgments on the French equivalents always confirm Wachowicz's judgments about (31), but I tend to give the same interpretation to (30) as to (31) at first, and if I think more about it, I lose intuitions but I don't seem to be able to get the interpretation that Wachowicz claims for (30). Other speakers of English I have interviewed have the same reaction to (30) and (31) as I have to the equivalent French examples. Very often also the possible interpretations have to be suggested to them, and they have to choose which sentence has which one of the suggested readings. My impression is that an interaction of factors may play a role in determining the (preferred) relative scope of the wh-phrases, for example, is the wh-phrase in Comp or not, what is its semantic role, what is its surface function, what is the (preferred) direction of the function? It is well-known that in the case of non-wh-quantifiers a variety of factors determine the preferred relative scope between them (Ioup, 1975) and that different speakers have different intuitions about existing readings (Carden, 1973). The same things might very well be at work in multiple questions. Just to give a last judgment about questions such as (30) and (31), let us quote Hull (1974:268):

> [(31)] presupposes merely that there were some girls who individually noticed some errors, with no restrictions as to how many errors a particular girl may have noticed nor any restriction as to how many girls may have noticed a particular error.

In fact, the difference between Wachowicz's and Hull's judgments may be rather easy to explain. For Wachowicz (30) is not ambiguous, and it is a function from girls to errors, while for me it seems to be a function from errors to girls. This suggests that (30) is potentially ambiguous and that we get or focus on one of the two readings only. It is then possible that Hull allows for both readings: this would be consistent with no apparent restrictions on the sorts of girls-errors pairings for him. I will thus assume that sentences like (30) and (31) are ambiguous and that some independent factors will eventually be found that will account for why some people select only one of the readings. Nothing really crucial depends on this for what follows.

I will discuss only one reading of (31), that in which we have a function from errors to girls, i.e. for each error only one girl noticed it, but it may be the case that some girls may have noticed several errors. I assume that nothing distinguishes a single from a multiple wh-question. Consider (26)a again. As we said, (27)a is the sort of answer expected, rather than (27)b:

(26) a. Which boy likes Mary?

(27) a. Peter likes Mary.

b. Peter and Fred like Mary.

There is no doubt that this is due to the fact that *which boy* is in the singular. Forgetting about this aspect for a second, we have seen that one could think of representing questions such as (26)a by (32):

(32) $\lambda P \hat{P}{}^{\vee}P(\hat{x}[boy(x) \ \& \ P\{x\}])(\verb|^|like'(\hat{P}P\{{}^{\wedge}m\}))$

(32) denotes a set containing the senses of possible term-denotations. The contribution of the singular here is that the question denotes the sense of one and only one individual concept. The problem is to incorporate this into the translation or to make it part of an implicature associated with (32) in such a way that it won't have any undesirable results in the case of multiple questions, as it has in Karttunen's analysis. I don't know the correct formal way to obtain the result I want and my account will consequently be in part informal.

Take question (28), and let us represent it by (33):

(33) $\lambda P_1 \lambda P_2 [{}^{\vee}P_2(\hat{x}[boy(x) \ \& \ [{}^{\vee}P_1(\hat{y}[girl(y) \ \& \ like'_*({}^{\vee}x,{}^{\vee}y)])]])]$

(33) denotes a set of ordered pairs, it is a function from girls to boys. We must ensure that for each relevant girl there is only one boy. Let us assume that we have a discourse with 4 boys, Fred, Bill, Paul, and Peter, and 4 girls, Anna, Sue, Mary, and Gwen. In the case of (32) only one argument, Peter, turned the function into a true proposition. In the case of (33), if we try the four possible girls separately, we can't check whether the expressions are true, because we still have functions, i.e. the four questions in (34):

(34) a. $\lambda P_2[{}^{\vee}P_2(\hat{x}[boy(x) \ \& \ girl'_*(a) \ \& \ like'_*({}^{\vee}x,a)])]$

b. $\lambda P_2[{}^{\vee}P_2(\hat{x}[boy(x) \ \& \ girl'_*(s) \ \& \ like'_*({}^{\vee}x,s)])]$

c. $\lambda P_2[{}^{\vee}P_2(\hat{x}[boy(x) \ \& \ girl'_*(m) \ \& \ like'_*({}^{\vee}x,m)])]$

d. $\lambda P_2[{}^{\vee}P_2(\hat{x}[boy(x) \ \& \ girl'_*(g) \ \& \ like'_*({}^{\vee}x,g)])]$

What the singular tells us, both in the case of (32) and (33) is that the set of properties of one particular individual concept will satisfy a certain expression; in (32) the final expression is given, but not in (33).

Depending on the choice of a girl, a choice of a particular boy will be made. One way to express the conditions imposed by (26)a and (28) would be as follows:

(35) a. With respect to a particular girl, Mary, there is one and only one boy who kissed her.

b. With respect to a particular girl, there is one and only one boy who kissed her.

In (35)a the girl is given. In (35)b, if there is only one girl who has been kissed, we will have a non-multiple answer; if different girls have been kissed, for each particular girl there will be only one boy. What we see is that depending on the facts in the world, we can look at a multiple question as an expression equivalent to one question (give me the only pair, triple, etc., such that...) or as an expression equivalent to a set of questions. In the second case, (28) is equivalent to (36):

(36) For each girl, which boy kissed her?

The only well worked out proposal at this time is Karttunen's (1977b), and it unfortunately leads to undesirable results. If a formal analysis along the lines we have suggested can be developed, it would give strong support for the sort of approach discussed until now.

FOOTNOTES TO CHAPTER III

1. Literally, this is incorrect, because it predicts that (i) is a possible answer to (3):

> (i) Peter and Fred are leaving in July and again in September.

What is meant is clear however.

2. This corresponds to the situation described by Hankamer (1974:73, fn.3):

> The asker of the question must have in mind some finite set of candidates for each WH to be specified, so that in effect he is asking his addressee to specify which of a finite set of possible circumstances, all visualized by him, obtains.... In any case all of the multiple questions discussed in this paper require such a presupposition; failure to construct one will make them all sound very strange.

3. Wachowicz has observed that several languages were sensitive to the distinction between known and unknown in multiple questions. For example, in Konkani when the values for a wh-word are known by the questioner, the wh-word is reduplicated; so we have the following examples:

> (i) a. kɔnɛ kəslẽ-kəslẽ ghɛtlẽ?
>
> who what-what bought?
>
> who bought what (known)?
>
> b. kɔnɛ-kɔnɛ kəslẽ-kəslẽ ghɛtlẽ?
>
> who-who what-what bought?
>
> who (known) bought what (known)?
>
> c. kɔnɛ-kɔnɛ kəslẽ ghɛtlẽ?
>
> who-who what bought?
>
> who (known) bought what?

This reduplication process is optional, and it was then impossible for Wachowicz to ascertain whether in the absence of reduplication multiple questions could be used when for none of the wh-words it was known what values it was going to take in the answer. She also noticed that in Polish and Russian all the wh-words could be fronted and that the leftmost one corresponded to known information. The distinction between known and unknown seems to play a role in French and English too.

If the judgments on the sentences below are correct, it seems that when we have a multiple question such that

1) the answer requires several pairings between elements drawn from two lists, and

2) the elements of one list have been specified, i.e. they have been mentioned and so are undoubtedly known by all participants in the discussion, but the elements of the other list haven't been mentioned and so it is possible that not all of the participants in the conversation know what they are (nobody may know that)

THEN the wh-word that is moved is the one that corresponds to the list of not mentioned elements. The judgments on the French examples are mine. Similar judgments were obtained about the English translations.

(ii) Pierre a tué Jean, François, et Luc (∅ vs dans différents endroits), et je sais même

   (a) OK où il a tué qui.

   (b) * qui il a tué où.

Peter killed John, Bill, and Fred (∅ vs in different places), and I even know

   (a) where he killed who.

   (b) * who he killed where.

(Try the same examples replacing et je sais même (and I even know) by mais je ne sais pas (but I don't know)).

(iii) Pierre a tué (quelqu'un vs des gens) à Paris, à Rome, et à Berlin, et je sais même

   (a) * où il a tué qui.

   (b) OK qui il a tué où.

(iii) continued

> Peter killed (somebody vs people) in Paris, Rome, and Berlin, and I even know
>
> (a) * *where* he killed *who*.
>
> (b) *who* he killed *where*.

With appropriate specification of contexts, some of these judgments can however be changed. Consider for example a discourse where it has been mentioned that crimes have been committed in Paris, Rome, and Berlin. Then I think that (ii)b becomes good. (ii)b was thus considered as bad because it was assumed that (ii)b was said in a context where the places were unknown. (ii)b becomes grammatical (appropriate) exactly where it is predicted, i.e. when it is known what *ou* stands for.

CHAPTER IV

KARTTUNEN'S ANALYSIS OF QUESTIONS

Karttunen (1977a, b) has proposed an interesting analysis of questions. It is not my purpose to study his proposals in detail here. I will limit myself to a short review of the main aspects of his analysis and point out the places where his analysis doesn't have problems of the sort we have seen in the second chapter. We will also examine the problem raised by multiple wh-questions with each wh-phrase in the singular and how Karttunen's analysis could be modified in a way that will account for the answers that such questions accept.

4.1 General Features of Karttunen's Analysis

In a way, the idea underlying Karttunen's analysis is similar to that discussed in the previous chapters: questions denote the set of their true answers (Karttunen, 1977a:11; see also Montague, 1974:248, fn. 3). The way Karttunen captures this is by letting questions denote sets of true propositions. This is a modification of Hamblin's analysis (1973), which lets questions denote sets of propositions that are possible answers.

4.1.1 Sets of propositions

Karttunen wants all questions to belong to the same syntactic category, and so to translate to expressions of intensional logic of the same logical type. This aspect of the analysis has various nice consequences. First of all, as Karttunen (1977a:5-6) points out, if wh-questions and whether-questions belong to different categories, a verb like *depend on* would have to be assigned to four different categories to generate examples like (1)a-d:

(1) a. Whether Mary comes depends on who invites her.

   b. Whether Mary comes depends on whether Max invites her.

   c. Who is elected depends on who is running.

   d. Who is elected depends on whether Connally is running.

As we saw, the analysis discussed in Chapter II requires even more than that, i.e. that each verb which takes questions belong to a theoretically infinite number of syntactic categories. It is however unclear whether this is a genuine problem rather than a problem simply resulting from the assumption that natural languages obey a theory of TYPES. And even if natural languages obey such a theory, that verbs taking questions would belong to a multiplicity of categories isn't necessarily a sign that the analysis forcing such a state of affairs is incorrect: the same problem arises in fact with a very large number of lexical items, according to Parsons (1977).

4.1.2 True propositions

Letting questions denote sets of TRUE propositions allows a straight-forward account of the intuition that in cases like (2) "the true answer to the question in the subject position depends on the true answer to the question in the object position" (Karttunen, 1977a:10). That the truth should be related to the wh-clauses themselves rather than to the verb is made clear by examples like (3) where the same verb is used, but no implication of truth is associated with the subject and the object:

(2) Who is elected depends on who is running.

(3) Whatever occurs in the subject position depends on whatever occurs in the object position.

Karttunen (1977a:11) makes the same point with the verb *tell*.

4.1.3 The performative analysis

Karttunen derives direct questions from indirect questions. I refer the reader to Karttunen himself (1977a:3-4) for a short discussion of that aspect. One of the consequences of this choice is that it allows him to account for the ambiguity of questions like (4) (Karttunen, 1977a:31-33):

(4) What grade does every student deserve?

These are the main aspects of Karttunen's analysis.

4.2 Single and Multiple Wh-questions

We have given in 2.2.6 examples of *yes-no* and of alternative questions translated according to Karttunen's analysis. No problem arises with such translations. In this section I will limit myself to one sort of wh-question that is a problem for Karttunen, multiple questions like (5):

(5) Which boy likes which girl?

Consider questions like (6) first:

(6) Which girl does John like?

Karttunen suggests associating with each natural language expression two expressions of intensional logic. One is the extension expression, and is identical to the single translation that is provided in most works done in Montague Grammar; the other is the implicature expression, and stands for the conventionally implicated meaning of each phrase. For details, see Karttunen (1977b) and Karttunen and Peters (1975, 1976). (6) conveys a uniqueness implicature, i.e. it conventionally implicates that John likes only one girl. The translation of (6) is then as in (7); the first part is the EXTENSION EXPRESSION, and is identical to the single translation that Montague would provide; the second is the IMPLICATURE EXPRESSION, and represents the conventionally implicated meaning of the translated phrase (I refer the reader to Karttunen (1977b) for the rules that are used to obtain these translations; here, the superscript 'e' is equivalent to the superscript '!' used earlier):

(7) $<\hat{p} \; \forall x[girl^e(x) \; \& \; {}^\vee p \; \& \; p = {}^\wedge like^e_*(j, {}^\vee x)];$

$\hat{p}(\forall x \wedge y[[girl^e(y) \; \& \; like^e_*(j, {}^\vee y)]$

$\rightarrow x = y] \; \& \; ...]>$

The second part of the translation says that there is only girl. When the same rules that are used to construct (7) are used to translate (5), the result is (8):

(8) $<\hat{p} \forall y \forall x[girl^e(y) \; \& \; boy^e(x) \; \& \; {}^\vee p \; \& \; p = {}^\wedge like^e_*({}^\vee x, {}^\vee y)];$

$\hat{p}[\forall y \wedge z[[girl^e(z) \; \& \; \forall x[boy^e(x) \; \& \; like^e_*({}^\vee x, {}^\vee z)]] \leftrightarrow z = y]$

$\forall y[girl^e(y) \; \& \; \forall x \wedge w[[boy^e(w) \; \& \; like^e_*({}^\vee w, {}^\vee y)] \leftrightarrow w = x]] \; \& ...]>$

The extension expression here denotes the set of true propositions of the form 'x likes y', where x ranges over boys and y over girls. The implicature expression amounts to saying that there is only one pair of a boy and a girl such that the boy likes the girl. This is not a good result. I don't see at this time how the details of Karttunen's analysis, especially in the case of the implicature expressions, should be modified so that the desired result is obtained both in single and multiple questions. One possibility however would be to treat the second (quantified in) wh-phrase as having the same translation as *every girl*, for example, so that the translation of (5) would be equivalent to that of (9):

(9) For every girl, I ask you to tell me which boy likes her.

This would, however, mean that wh-phrases in questions would have different translations according to when they are introduced: the first one would be translated as Karttunen does as an existentially quantified NP, the others as universally quantified NP's. If the second wh-phrase is translated as *every N*, no uniqueness implicature would be associated with it. But the second wh-phrase and the next ones couldn't be quantified in into the questions directly. If we did that, leaving implicatures aside, the translation of (5) would be (10):

(10) $\beta \wedge y[girl'(y) \rightarrow \forall x[boy'(x) \ \& \ ^{\vee}p \ \& \ p=\ ^{\wedge}like_*^!(^{\vee}x,^{\vee}y)]]$

As noted by Karttunen (1977a:31, fn. 15) in his discussion of questions of the type of (11) discussed earlier, in a world where there is more than one girl, a formula like (10) denotes the null set.

(11) What grade does every student deserve?

It is thus inappropriate to represent the meaning of questions like (5) by (10). This means that if we wanted to maintain that the second quantified in wh-phrase is a universally quantified phrase, it would have to be quantified in in the manner that *every N* is quantified in, i.e. not directly in the set of propositions, but in an expression of type t. This would lead to syntactic complications: a wh-phrase could be quantified in into a t-phrase, with exactly the same semantic effect as when *every N* is quantified in into a t-phrase, only if it will interact in a certain way with another wh-phrase. I won't attempt to specify this interaction, since the analysis looks rather unattractive to me, at least in the form that I have suggested.[1]

If it is not possible to account for both single and multiple wh-questions of the type of (6) and (5) in a parallel way within Karttunen's general hypothesis that questions denote sets of true propositions, the general approach will have to be questioned, just as the approach examined in detail in Chapter II will be difficult to support if the problems raised there can't be solved in a satisfactory way.

FOOTNOTE TO CHAPTER IV

1. Using both existential and universal quantifiers to describe the meaning of questions was proposed already by Hintikka (1974, 1976). Hintikka assumes that these quantifiers should be used in both single and multiple wh-questions. Hintikka (1974:129) tries to support his analysis with some facts involving multiple questions in Finnish:

> As a reminder of this close relationship between quantifiers and the WH-element, we may use the observation that one of them can occasionally do the same job in one language as the other in another. A case in point is the English question
>
> Where is each of you coming from?
>
> It may be translated into Finnish as follows:
>
> Mistä kukin teistä tulee?
>
> Here the job of the 'quantifier' *each* is taken over by the interrogative *kukin*.

The point is clearer and better made by Wachowicz (1974:39), when she tries to provide evidence that in multiple questions, "each of the sets for which the wh-words stand must have at least two members":

> Finnish furnishes further support for this claim. Genuine multiple questions must have the particle *-kin* attached to the last wh-word. The meaning of this particle is 'each', e.g. *kuka* 'who' becomes 'who-each' *kukin*- after the attachment of this particle; *mitä* 'what' becomes 'what-each' *-mitäkin*. The meaning of 'each' seems to exclude the possibility that n=1, i.e. each of the wh-words would stand for a set which contains only one member. If it were possible to have a single n-tuple as a proper answer to a multiple question, Finnish should make a distinction between multiple Wh-questions that have a single n-tuple as a proper answer versus those multiple Wh-questions which require a conjunction of n-tuples. In other words, these two types of multiple questions could be distinguished in Finnish in terms of the particle *-kin*. However, multiple questions which do not have the particle *-kin* can be interpreted in Finnish only as echo-questions....

From a brief discussion with Lauri Carlson, it seems however that it is possible to have the equivalent of (i) without -*kin* and as a genuine question, i.e. not as an echo question:

(i) Who hit who first?

If this is correct it would argue against Wachowicz's view and maybe also against the view that the second quantified in wh-phrase corresponds always to a universal quantifier, but not against the view that both existential and universal quantifiers play a role in the semantics of questions. But the facts mentioned by Hintikka and Wachowicz don't necessarily show that wh-phrases in multiple questions involve universal quantification. Frances and Lauri Karttunen (1975) present an analysis of -*kin* limited to its use in the sense of *also*, *too*. They show that -*kin* doesn't play a role in determining the truth conditions of sentences but that it contributes a conventional implicature to the sentence in which it occurs. For example, (ii)a and (ii)b express the same proposition, but in addition (ii)c may be inferred from (ii)a: by asserting (ii)a, the speaker commits himself to (ii)b and (ii)c.

(ii) a. Jussi pitaa Marjastakin. 'Jussi likes MARJA too.'

b. Jussi pitaa Marjasta. 'Jussi likes Marja.'

c. Jussi pitaa jostakin muusta kuin Marjasta.
   'Jussi likes someone other than Marja.'

The implicature associated with -*kin* is thus something like:

(iii) There is an x other than y which...

The contribution of -*kin* when attached to an interrogative pronoun is not discussed, but it seems likely that the implicature that they propose for -*kin* when cliticized to a non-questioned NP will be enough to account for the cases where -*kin* is cliticized to an interrogative pronoun. In an example such as Hintikka's above, the implication will roughly be that there is some x other than y who is coming from some place, i.e. there is more than one pairing of an individual with some place.

CHAPTER V

ITERATED MULTIPLE QUESTIONS AND SCOPE AMBIGUITIES

5.0 Introduction

In this chapter we will discuss questions like (1) which, following Hintikka (1974), we will refer to as iterated multiple questions.

(1) Who knows where Mary bought which book?

Most linguists and philosophers who have studied iterated multiple questions such as (1) have argued that they are ambiguous between narrow scope and wide scope reading for *which book*; from now on we will generally simply talk about the narrow scope and the wide scope reading of the question.

On the narrow scope reading, the request for information concerns only the subject of the main clause; the person who asks the question wants to know which values have to be substituted for x in (2) in order for (2) to become a true sentence:

(2) x knows where Mary bought which book.

(3) would be the sort of answer expected to such a reading of (1):

(3) Peter, Paul, and Mary do.

On the wide scope reading the speaker wants to know which values have to be substituted for x and y in (4) in order for it to become a true sentence:

(4) x knows where Mary bought y.

(5) would be the sort of answer expected to such a reading of (1):

(5) Peter knows where Mary bought *Aspects* and Paul knows where Mary bought *Syntactic Structures*, and Fred knows where Mary bought *Structural Linguistics*.

For the specific purpose of this chapter it makes no difference if we decide to represent the two readings of (1) along the lines of the analysis of questions discussed in Chapters II and III, i.e. as in (6)a and (6)b, with $^vP_1$ for *who*, $^vP_2$ for *which book*, and a^1 a variable over locative adverbs, or along the lines of Karttunen,[1] as in (7)a and (7)b, or along the lines of Williams (1977) and May (1977), as in (8)a and (8)b, where t_n is a trace left by wh-movement or wh-interpretation.

(6) a. $\lambda P_1[{}^\vee P_1({}^\wedge know'({}^\wedge \lambda a^1 \lambda P_2[\ m* \ ({}^\wedge a^1(\ buy'(P_2))))])))]$

  b. $\lambda P_2 \lambda P_1[{}^\vee P_1({}^\wedge know'({}^\wedge \lambda a^1[\ m* \ ({}^\wedge a^1({}^\wedge buy'(P_2)))])))]$

(7) a. $\hat{q} \ Vz \ [{}^\vee q \ \& \ q = {}^\wedge know'(z, \hat{p} \ Vy \ Vx \ [book'(y) \ \& \ place'(x) \ \&$
    $\ {}^\vee p \ \& \ p = {}^\wedge buy'_*(m, {}^\vee y, {}^\vee x)])]$

  b. $\hat{q} \ Vy \ Vz[book'(y) \ \& \ {}^\vee q \ \& \ q = {}^\wedge know'(z, \hat{p} \ Vx \ [place'(x) \ \&$
    $\ {}^\vee p \ \& \ p = {}^\wedge buy'_*(m, {}^\vee y, {}^\vee x)])]$

(8) a. [who$_i$ [t$_i$ knows [what$_j$ [where$_k$ [we bought t$_j$ t$_k$]]]]]
    $\overline{S}$ S $\overline{S}$ $\overline{S}$ S

  b. [what$_j$ [who$_i$ [t$_i$ knows [where$_k$ [we bought t$_j$ t$_k$]]]]]
    $\overline{S}$ $\overline{S}$ S $\overline{S}$ S

In most cases I will make use of the last kind of representation. One reason for this is that we will discuss some sentences for which the details of the analysis within Montague Grammar have not been fully worked out. Except for these details, there is no difficulty in going from the representations of the type of (8) to those of the type of (7) and (6). The other reason is that much of the discussion here will draw on Williams (1977): adopting his notation will make the reading easy for those already familiar with his work. In some cases where the details of the semantics are crucial we will use representations such as in (6).

Although it is generally assumed that sentences like (1) are ambiguous, Kuno and Robinson (1972) have argued that they are not, that they only have the narrow scope reading. So, in their analysis, (5) is not the direct answer to the question, and they claim that the fact that it is considered as an acceptable reply to (1) should be explained in pragmatic terms. Hankamer (1974) criticizes several aspects of Kuno and Robinson's work. He shows that the constraint that they propose and which predicts that sentences like (1) have only the narrow scope reading doesn't exist and that their analysis predicts several sorts of replies to be acceptable when in fact they are not. I have tried to show elsewhere (Hirschbühler, 1977) that it is, however, still possible to argue that (1) is not ambiguous and

that Hankamer's objections can be answered. And Kuno and Robinson
also present several cases in favor of their analysis that are not
discussed by Hankamer. Here I will argue that the traditional
view is correct, i.e. that (1) is ambiguous, considering facts
that generally haven't been discussed.

5.1 Kuno and Robinson's analysis and a modified version of it

Kuno and Robinson's representation of the deep structure of (1)
is similar to (9)[2]:

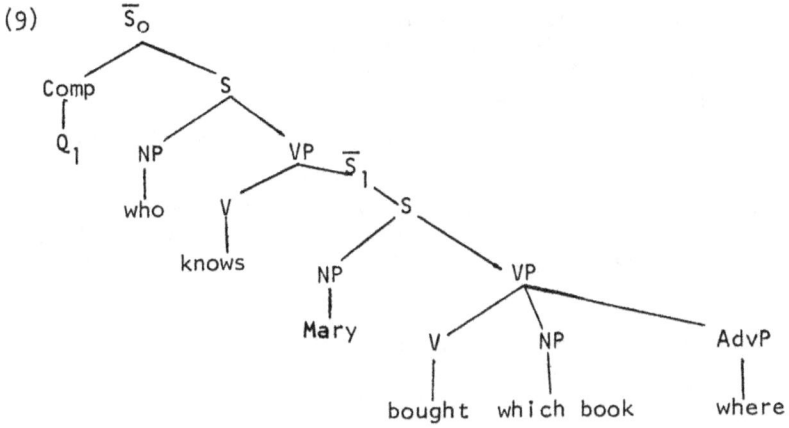

Kuno and Robinson's position is based on two observations (1972:
480). First, they note that other constituents than wh's that some
take as having widest scope (in their terms, matrix-Q-bound wh-words)
can be specified, can be given some value, in the reply. Second,
they note that "there are nonlinguistic circumstances under which
giving constant values only to the matrix-Q-bound wh's would yield
counterfactual answers".

The first point is exemplified by a question like (10) which
can have (3) and (5) as acceptable replies, just as (1) can.

(10) Who knows where we bought these books?

The fact that *these books* is given constant values in the reply
has never been taken as indicating that *these books* was bound by Q,
and similarly, the fact that *which book* in (1) is given constant
values in (5) doesn't force one to say that *which book* is bound
by the matrix Q (Kuno and Robinson, 1972:481).

The second point is based on the observation that there are circumstances under which (3) can be false and (5) true. They propose the following general principle to account for the existence of replies like (3) and (5) to questions like (1), assuming that such questions are not ambiguous and have only a reading as in (8)a:

(11) We hold that giving more information than is syntactically called for, namely giving constant values to wh-words or other variables (such as *these books*) that are not bound by the matrix Q is possible only when assigning constant values to the matrix-Q-bound alone would constitute a counterfactual or inaccurate answer.

(Kuno and Robinson, 1972:480)

To ensure that sentences like (1) cannot be ambiguous, i.e. to mechanically restrict the scope of the unmoved wh-word, Kuno and Robinson (1972:471) propose the Clause Mate Constraint on Multiple Wh-words:

(12) Multiple wh-words bound by the same Q must be clause mates at the time of application of wh-Q movement.

Hankamer (1974) has shown that there was no such constraint, otherwise examples like the following good one would have to be marked as ungrammatical:

(13) What I can't remember is WHICH RECIPE requires that I buy WHICH SPICE.

Kuno and Robinson's constraint can however be replaced by a more adequate one like (14) if one wants to allow examples such as (13) and still prevent (1) from having a reading such as in (8)b.

(14) Scope of unmoved wh rule:

Unmoved question-words must be bound by the first Q that commands them.

Such a principle would also account for examples such as (15) which have nearly always been given as ungrammatical in the literature (but see our discussion in 5.4) and for examples such as (16)a,b:

(15) *Who remembers whether John kissed who?

(16) a. Which books are you not sure whether or not you should read?

b. Which books are you not sure whether to read?

We will come back to sentences such as (15) in 5.4. Without additional mechanism, a theory which allows unmoved wh-words to take different scopes when the conditions for it exist predicts that (15) will be grammatical under the wide scope reading.

Before discussing some cases supporting the view that iterated multiple questions are ambiguous, let us quickly mention that Kuno and Robinson fail to consider the possibility that not only the scope of unmoved wh-words could be taken into account in explaining why (3) and (5) are considered as possible adequate replies to questions such as (1), but also the scope of non wh-words: everybody agrees that in (10) *these books* could not be bound by the Q postulated for the matrix sentence, but there is no a priori reason that *these books* cannot have scope over the whole sentence anyway.

5.2 Evidence for the ambiguity of iterated questions

The traditional argument for the ambiguity of questions like (1) is based on the existence of different kinds of appropriate replies. This alone is however not enough to show that such questions are ambiguous since Kuno and Robinson claim that the existence of these different kinds of replies can be accounted for even if (1) is not ambiguous and had only the narrow scope reading. In the following sections we will see that by constructing questions in a certain way it is possible to eliminate one or the other kind of answer, i.e. the narrow scope or the wide scope reading of the question. The fact that we can force one kind of answer just by manipulating the question, not the context, is evidence that we are dealing with meanings of questions, rather than with pragmatics.

5.2.1 Iterated questions and VP interpretation

Sentences missing VP's on the surface have properties which can easily be explained if sentences like (1) are ambiguous. Consider for example the following dialogues.

(17) a. A - Who knows where we bought which book?

b. B - Peter, Paul, and Mary do.

c. A - And who already did yesterday?

d. B - Peter (did).

(18) a. A - Who knows where we bought which book?

b. B - Well, Peter knows where we bought *Aspects*, and Sue knows where we bought *Syntactic Structures*, and Fred knows where we bought *Roots*.

c. A - *And who did yesterday?

c'. A - *And which one of them already did yesterday?

c''. A - *And who else will tomorrow?

(19) a. Who knows where we bought which book and

(i) who else will tomorrow?

(ii) who already did yesterday?

b. Peter, Paul, and Mary, and (i) Fred will tomorrow.

(ii) Peter already did yesterday.

c. *Peter knows where we bought *Aspects*, Paul knows where we bought *Syntactic Structures*, Mary knows where we bought *Structural Linguistics*, and Fred will tomorrow.

The fact that the VP is missing in the second conjunct of (19)a eliminates the possibility of replies like (19)c; the fact that the answer to (18)a is a multiple one prevents the question (18)c from being appropriate. It is not clear at all what those facts would follow from under Kuno and Robinson's approach. But they can be explained if we assume that sentences like (1) are ambiguous and if we adopt Williams' (1977) theory of VP interpretation. Williams proposes that we take what is generally called the VP deletion rule to be an interpretive rule which takes as input logical forms rather than syntactic structures. This view is a consequence of where in the grammar VP interpretation takes place and where rules such as wh-interpretation and quantifier interpretation take place. I will quickly present the aspects of Williams' analysis of VP interpretation that are necessary for our purpose.

According to Williams, a grammar of a language contains, among others, the following components:

1. A sentence grammar component.

2. A discourse grammar component.

The sentence grammar component operates before the discourse grammar component. Among the components of sentence grammar, Williams argues that we have the following ones, in order:

1. Base rule component (generates deep structure)

2. Transformational component (maps deep structures into surface structures)

3. Semantic interpretation component (takes surface structures to give the logical form of the sentence; the rules of quantifier interpretation and of wh-interpretation are rules that belong to that component).

Rules that can operate across utterance boundaries, such as VP interpretation, are rules of discourse grammar. They have to follow rules of semantic interpretation. For the problem which we examine here, three rules have to be considered:

1. Wh-movement

2. Wh-scope assignment

3. VP-interpretation

Wh-movement moves a wh-phrase in COMP, leaving a trace. We assume with Williams that the rule of wh-scope assignment is a rule of sentence grammar and that it is formulated as in (20):

(20) $[\text{wh}_i\ldots\text{wh}_j\ldots]_{\bar{S}} \rightarrow [\text{wh}_j\ [\text{wh}_i\ldots t_j\ldots]]_{\bar{S}\ \bar{S}}$

Before examining how those rules interact in the case of examples like (17)-(19), consider first the following sentences and their simplified representation (tense is systematically left out):

(21) a. What did you buy?

b. $[\ [\text{what}_1]\ [\text{you}\ [\text{buy}\ t_1]]]$
    $\bar{S} \qquad\quad S \quad\ VP$

(22) a. Where did you buy what?

b. [what₁ [where₂ [you [buy t₁ t₂]]]]
   S̄   S̄   S   VP

(23) a. Who bought this book?

b. [who₁ [t₁ [buy this book]]]
   S̄   S   VP

We may observe now that the equivalent of (21)-(23) with an empty VP site is ungrammatical, i.e. we have:

(24) a. *What did you buy and what did Peter?

b. *I wonder what you bought and what Peter did.

(25) a. *Where did you buy what and where did Peter?

b. *I wonder where you bought what and where Peter did.

but:

(26) Who bought this book today and who did yesterday?
(just assume that it is a book which is resold every day.)

Why things are so is clear within Williams' theory. Consider (24)a first. After wh-scope assignment the logical form looks like (27)a; then the rule of VP-interpretation applies. This rule copies the antecedent VP (we omit here such rules as Williams' (1977:section 2, and 1.5.3) derived VP and f-subscripting rules).

(27) a. [what₁ [you [buy t₁]]] and [what₂ [Peter [   ]]]
        S̄   S   VP   S̄   S   VP

b. [what₁ [you [buy t₁]]] and [what₂ [Peter [buy t₁]]]

A trace is properly bound by a binding phrase if it is c-commanded, and preceded by it (May, 1977:21).

We are now in a position to see what is wrong with (24)a, whose logical form is (27)b after VP-interpretation has applied. In the second conjunct of (27)b, t_1 is unbound, since $what_1$ in the first conjunct doesn't c-command it. In addition $what_2$ doesn't bind any trace and it won't, as a consequence, be interpreted as an argument of *buy*. The same comment is true about (25), whose representation after wh-interpretation and VP-interpretation is given in (28):

(28)   [$what_1$ [$where_2$[you [buy $t_1 t_2$]]]] and [$where_3$ [Peter [buy $t_1 t_2$]]]

Here, in the second conjunct, neither t_1 nor t_2 is properly bound, and $where_3$ doesn't bind any trace. The fact that in these cases we will have a wh-phrase which won't be assigned any function is enough to exclude them. In addition, the sentences may be excluded if, as we suggested in 2.2.2.1, different occurences of the same variable must be treated alike: the unbound traces which will be turned into variables when the logical forms will be translated in some logical language won't be able to be treated as free variables assigned some value with respect to the context, because there will be occurences of the same variable that will be bound. These variables will thus be uninterpreted. We claim then that uninterpreted variables in a formula make that formula ill-formed.

We are ready now to examine iterative questions. Consider (19)a first:

(19)a.   Who knows where we bought which book and who already did yesterday?

On the narrow scope reading, the representation for (19)a after application of wh-interpretation is (29)a and this is turned into (29)b by VP-interpretation:

(29)a. [who_1 [t_1 [knows [which $book_2$ [$where_3$ [we[bought t_2 t_3]]]]]]]
       $\bar{S}$ S   VP $\bar{S}$ $\bar{S}$ S   VP

       and [who_4 [t_4 did [   ] yesterday]]
            $\bar{S}$ S   VP

(29)b. [$_{\bar{S}}$ who$_1$ [$_S$ t$_1$ [$_{VP}$ knows [$_{\bar{S}}$ which book$_2$ [$_{\bar{S}}$ where$_3$ [$_S$ we [$_{VP}$ bought t$_2$ t$_3$]]]]]]]

and [$_{\bar{S}}$ who$_4$ [$_{\bar{S}}$ t$_4$ did [$_{VP}$ know [$_{\bar{S}}$ which book$_2$ [$_{\bar{S}}$ where$_3$ [$_S$ we [$_{VP}$ bought t$_2$ t$_3$]]]]]]yesterday]]

All variables are properly bound and each indexed wh-phrase properly binds a variable. We will now see that there is no way to get a well-formed wide scope reading for *which book* in (19)a.

(30)a is the logical form of (19)a with wide scope reading for *which book* and (30)b results from the application of VP-interpretation to (30)a:

(30)a. [$_{\bar{S}}$ which book$_1$ [$_{\bar{S}}$ who$_2$ [$_S$ t$_2$ [$_{VP}$ knows [$_{\bar{S}}$ where$_3$ [$_S$ we [$_{VP}$ bought t$_1$ t$_3$]]]]]]]

and [$_{\bar{S}}$ who$_4$ [$_S$ t$_4$ did [$_{VP}$] yesterday]]

Only the second conjunct after the application of VP-interpretation is given:

(30)b. [who$_4$ [t$_4$ did [know [where$_3$ [we [bought t$_1$ t$_3$]]]] yesterday]]

In (30)b, the trace t$_1$ in the embedded clause is not bound by any phrase; *which book*$_1$ is in the first conjunct and doesn't c-command t$_1$. The sentence is thus not well-formed. Under the hypothesis that sentences like (1) are ambiguous, we are thus able to provide an explanation for why a single answer to (19)a is possible, while a multiple one is not.

Let us turn now to examples like (18). As can be seen, (18)c is ungrammatical. This suggests first that the empty VP in (18)c can't take any of the VP's in (18)b as antecedent. This could perhaps be due to the fact that it is impossible to tell which one of the three VP's would be the antecedent. (18)a could provide the antecedent for the empty VP. But if we assume that an answer like (18)b indicates that (18)a is to be analyzed with widest scope for *which book*, then after the logical form of the VP of (18)a has been copied into (18)c, the result will be as in (30)b, which, as we have already seen, is not well-formed. The hypothesis that (1) is ambiguous together with Williams' analysis of VP interpretation allows us to account for why (18)c is bad as a continuation of (18)a and for why (19)c is not a possible answer to (19)a, while (19)b is.

Further support both for the hypothesis that (1) is ambiguous and for Williams' analysis can be found in cases where only the VP of the embedded question is missing; in that case we find the opposite judgments i.e., only the multiple answer is appropriate and the non-multiple one is not. We thus have the following facts:

(31) a. Who knows which boy subscribes to which magazine and which girl does too?

b. Peter knows which boy subscribes to *Playboy* and which girl does too and Fred knows which boy subscribes to *Playgirl* and which girl does too.

c. *Peter knows which boy subscribes to which magazine and which girl does too.

Notice that given that (31)c is ungrammatical, just as the direct question (32), the grammaticality of (31)a would be difficult to explain if *which magazine* didn't have scope over the whole sentence.

(32) *Which boy subscribes to which magazine and which girl does too?

If in (31)a, *which magazine* has widest scope, it will be represented as in (33), after VP copying has applied:

70 - Hirschbühler

(33)

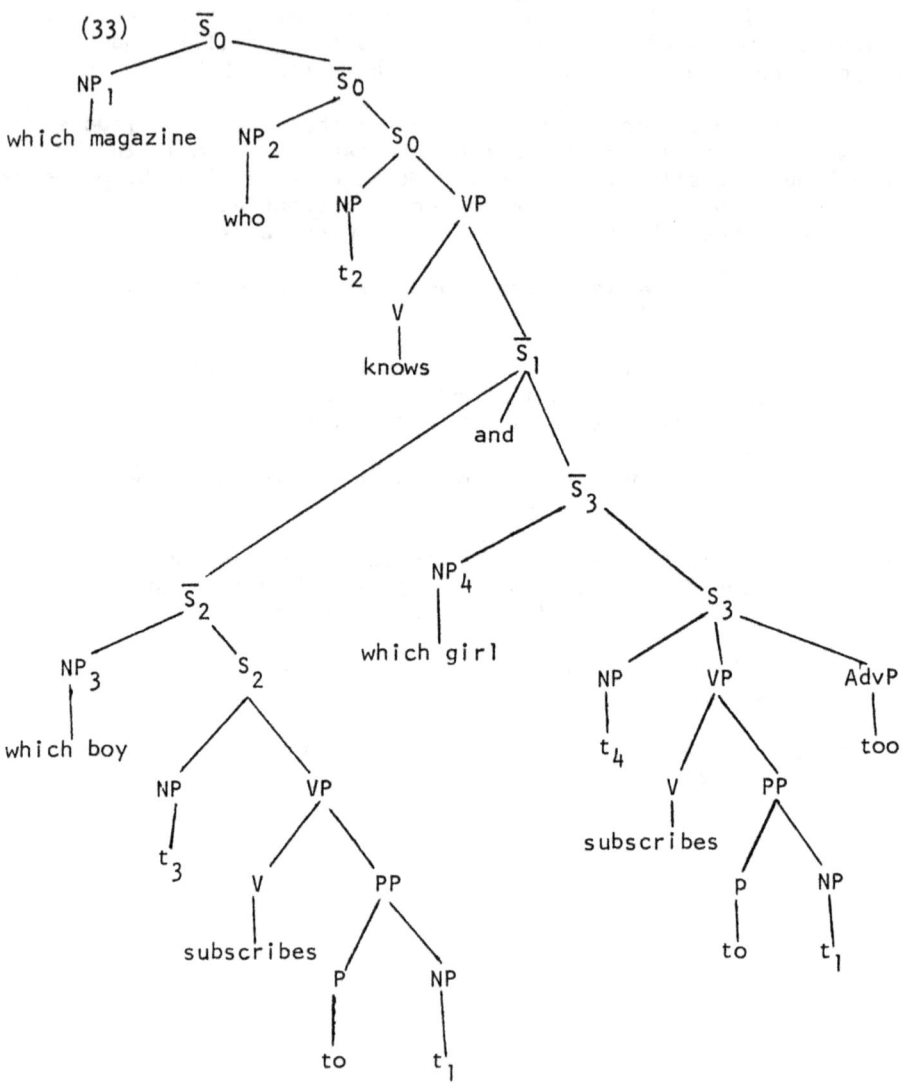

One can see that the trace t_1 in S_3 is properly bound by *which magazine*$_1$ since it is c-commanded by it. One can also check that if *which magazine*$_1$ was under the domination of $\bar{S}_2$, the trace t_1 in S_3 would not be properly bound. The theory also predicts that (34) is ungrammatical, even when *which magazine* has widest scope.

(34) *Who knows which boy subscribes to which magazine and which girl does too, and who already did [know] yesterday?

What is going to be copied in the last empty VP is something like (35), assuming that VP copying has applied to the first empty VP first:

(35) knows which boy subscribes to x and which girl subscribes to x too.

The two x's in the first empty VP are going to be properly bound by *which magazine*, but they are not going to be properly bound in the next sentence, which is coordinated to the main clause. (34) is indeed ungrammatical. Notice that the ungrammaticality is not simply a matter of complexity, since (36) is good:

(36) Who knows which boy subscribes to *Playboy* and which girl does too, and who already did yesterday?

Finally, it is possible to construct examples with a missing VP where the ambiguity is preserved, because after VP-copying has applied, all the traces are properly bound, as is the case with (37), with tentative answers (38)-(40):

(37) Which girl discovered where we bought which book before which boy did? [discover where....]

The judgments on the tentative answers are delicate because the sentence is complex, but most of them seem to be as follows:

(38) a. Mary did before Alan did.

b. Mary did before Alan did, and Sue did before Peter (did).

(39) Mary discovered where we bought *Syntactic Structures* before Alan did, and Sue discovered where we bought *Aspects* before Fred did.

(40) *Mary discovered where we bought *Aspects* before Alan discovered where we bought *Syntactic Structures*, and Sue discovered where we bought *Structural Linguistics* before Fred discovered where we bought *Language and Mind*.

(38)a-b are answers to the narrow scope reading; (39) is an answer to the wide scope reading.

The syntactic structure of (37) is given in (41)[3]:

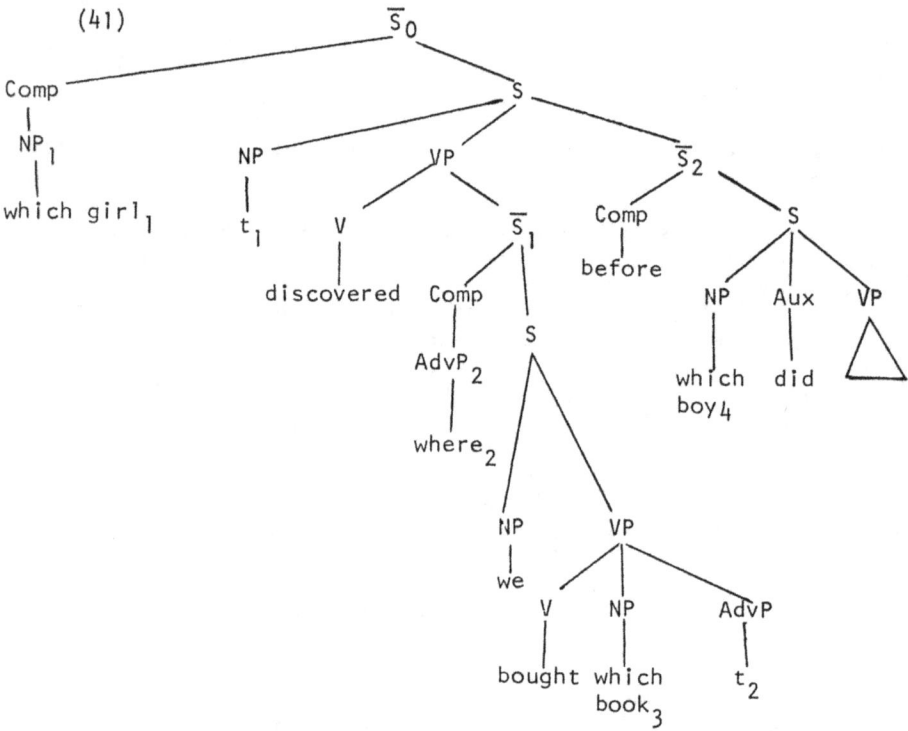

Application of wh-scope assignment to (41) with *which book*$_3$ given narrow scope gives us the following logical form:

(42) [which boy$_4$ [which girl$_1$ [t$_1$ [discovered [which book$_3$
    $\overline{S}$ $\overline{S}$ S   VP $\overline{S}$

[where$_2$ [we [bought t$_2$ t$_3$]]]]] [before [t$_4$ did [   ]]]]]]
$\overline{S}$ S   VP $\overline{S}$ S   VP

Application of the VP-interpretation rule gives us (43), which is well-formed:

(43) [which boy$_4$ [which girl$_1$ [t$_1$[discovered [which book$_3$
      $\bar{S}$ $\bar{S}$ S VP $\bar{S}$

      [where$_2$[we [bought t$_2$ t$_3$]]]]] [before [t$_4$ did [discover
      $\bar{S}$ S VP $\bar{S}$ S   VP

      [which book$_3$ [where$_2$[we [bought t$_2$ t$_3$]]]]]]]]]]
      $\bar{S}$ $\bar{S}$ S VP

In (43), every trace is properly bound, in particular t$_3$. Since this is the narrow scope reading for *which book*$_3$, the existence of answers like (38)a and (38)b is accounted for.

In the case of the wide scope reading of (37), the syntactic surface structure is as in (41) too, but this time application of wh-scope assignment gives (44):

(44)   [which boy$_4$ [which book$_3$ [which girl$_1$ [t$_1$ [discovered
       $\bar{S}$ $\bar{S}$ $\bar{S}$ S   VP

       [where$_2$ [we [bought t$_2$ t$_3$]]]] [before [t$_4$ did
       $\bar{S}$ S   VP $\bar{S}$ S

       [   ]]]]]]]
       VP

VP-copying gives (45):

(45)   [which boy$_4$ [which book$_3$ [which girl$_1$ [t$_1$ [discovered
       $\bar{S}$ $\bar{S}$ $\bar{S}$ S   VP

       [where$_2$ [we [bought t$_2$t$_3$]]]] [before [t$_4$ did
       $\bar{S}$ S   VP $\bar{S}$ S

       [discover [where$_2$ [we [bought t$_2$ t$_3$]]]]]]]]]
         VP $\bar{S}$ S   VP

Every trace in (45), in particular t_4 and t_3, is properly bound. Answers like (39) are thus predicted to be possible. The impossibility of (42) is easy to explain: different occurences of the same variable must have the same value: *which book*$_3$ binds two occurences of t_3 in (45); in the answer the values for different occurences of the variable corresponding to t_3 must be the same.

We will conclude this section on VP-interpretation here. The hypothesis that questions like (1) are ambiguous and that the ambiguity should be represented as in (8)a-b (or as in (6)a-b, (7)a-b) together with Williams' analysis of VP-interpretation enables us to account easily for what answers to questions with missing VP's are possible. I see no way that an analysis along the lines of Kuno and Robinson can account for the same facts. In the next section, further support for the ambiguity of sentences like (1) will be found in questions containing cleft sentences.

5.2.2 Iterated questions and cleft sentences

In this section we will see how the clefting of the moved wh-phrase affects the range of possible answers to iterated multiple questions.

Observe the contrast between (46)a and (46)b-c:

(46) a. I wonder who bought what.

   b. *I wonder who it is that bought what.

   c. *I wonder who John thinks it is that bought what.

The facts can be described as follows: an unmoved wh-phrase cannot have scope over a sentence over which a clefted wh-phrase has scope.[4] Notice also that it makes no difference whether the moved wh-phrase is in the Comp closest to the focus position of the cleft sentence or whether it is farther away.

Consider now the following iterative question:

(47) Who knows where it was that we bought what?

Although the embedded question in (47) has the same form as the embedded question in (46)b, the sentence is grammatical. (47) can however receive only a multiple answer of the sort given in (48); a non-multiple answer as in (49) is ungrammatical here.

(48) Well, John knows where it was that we bought *Aspects*, and Peter knows where it was that we bought *Syntactic Structures*.

(49) *John knows where it was that we bought what.

Both the fact that (47) is grammatical and the fact that it allows for an answer like (48), while (49) is ungrammatical, suggest that (47) has only the wide scope reading, i.e. that in which *what* has scope over the sentence over which *who* has scope. Notice that just as (46)c is ungrammatical, (50) is grammatical only with *what* taking widest scope. So an answer like (51)a to (50) is good while one like (51)b is not:

(50) Who knows where John thinks it is that we bought what?

(51) a. Peter knows where John thinks it is that we bought the table and Fred knows where John thinks it is that we bought the sofa.

b. *Peter knows where John thinks it is that we bought what.

Let us turn now to examples where the wh-phrase in the main clause is clefted. If sentences like (1) are ambiguous, and if clefting a wh-phrase prevents that wh-phrase from entering into a multiple question, then it is predicted that examples like (52) will accept answers like (53)a but not answers like (53)b. The prediction is correct.

(52) Who is it that knows where we bought what?

(53) a. It's John that knows where we bought what.

b. Well, it's John that knows where we bought the table and Fred that knows where we bought the sofa.

And as expected, if each of the moved wh-phrases is clefted, the sentence is ungrammatical:

(54) *Who is it that knows where it is that we bought what?

The assumption that (1) is ambiguous and that clefting affects some potential reading allows us to account correctly for these facts. It is unclear that any sort of explanation could be found under different assumptions.

5.2.3 Ungrammatical narrow scope reading

Consider sentences like (55):

(55) Who has forgotten how we interpret which of these formulas?[5]

A possible context for (55) would be a professor asking his teaching assistant about the students. What is interesting is that if we force a narrow scope reading for *which of these formulas*, the sentence is ungrammatical:[6]

(56) a. *Peter has forgotten how we interpret which of these formulas.

b. *Has anyone forgotten how we interpret which of these formulas?

c. *How do we interpret which of these formulas?

For some reason, *how* and a partitive wh-phrase can't be paired. But *who* and a partitive wh-phrase can:[7]

(57) Who can interpret which one of these formulas?

(57) must for example be considered in a situation where there are a certain number of formulas on the blackboard and a certain number of students, and it is known that for each formula exactly one student understands it, but the appropriate pairing is not known.

As expected, multiple answers to questions like (55) are good:

(58) Well, Peter has forgotten how we interpret formula 11, and Paul...how we interpret formula 14, and Mary... how we interpret formula 17.

If we adopt Kuno and Robinson's analysis, it is once again unclear why (55) is good and (56) is not. Under the ambiguity hypothesis, given the impossibility of pairing *how* and a partitive wh-phrase, we have a straightforward explanation for the contrast between (55) and (56).

Other facts confirm that scope possibilities play a role here (rather than the mere presence of *who* in (55)). For example, given what we have seen earlier, we predict that the equivalent of (55) in the second conjunct of a coordinated sentence with an empty VP will be ungrammatical, thus eliminating the wide scope reading:

(59) *Who has forgotten how we interpret which of these formulas, and who already had yesterday / who else will very soon?

Similarly, what we have seen about clefts predicts that (60)b is ungrammatical:

(60) a. Who has forgotten how it is that we interpret which of these formulas?

  b. *Who was it that had forgotten how we interpret which of these formulas?

Although we have found speakers who did not like (60)a we have never seen the reverse judgments, i.e. (60)a ungrammatical, and (60)b grammatical.

5.2.4 Wide scope reading "contextually" preferred

Finally there are cases of sentences which are ambiguous, but given the context, the wide scope reading is clearly the one intended. The first such example of this kind was brought to my attention by Irene Heim.

Imagine the following situation. Some well-known criminals are convicted for several murders. They want to get rid of all the witnesses before their trial begins and so they want to find out who the witnesses or witness for each murder were/was. One of them may thus ask the following, in order to make a list of the people to eliminate:

(61) Who knows where we killed which person?

From the context it is clear that he is not interested in knowing simply who is a witness to all the crimes. A similar question may be asked by the prosecutor in the preparation for the trial:

(62) Who knows where they killed each person?

The next two cases were given me by Barbara Hall Partee.

Imagine a graduate student without a dissertation topic, and who still doesn't know in what area to work. He may ask his advisor the following question:

(63) Who has the best idea(s) of how to pursue
  {which thesis topic?
  {what sort of thesis topic?

Or in a situation where each course in a department has to be evaluated by somebody from outside (a different judge for each specialty), the person who has to put together an evaluation committee may ask:

(64) Who would be the best judge on how to evaluate which course?

Here too the intended meaning is clearly similar to that found in (65):

(65) For each course, who is the best judge on how to evaluate it?

Consider also the following dialogues, where we try to force one reading and then the other. If each dialogue is good, it means that sentences like (1) are ambiguous. And each dialogue is good.

(66) A. Who remembers where we bought which book?

B. John does.

A. Good, now I finally know who remembers where we bought which book.

(67) a. A - Who remembers where we bought which book?

b. B - Peter remembers where we bought *Aspects* and Sue remembers where we bought *Syntactic Structures*, and Fred remembers where we bought *Structural Linguistics*.

c. A - Good, now I finally know who remembers where we bought which book.

The crucial case is (67). If in (67)c *which book* couldn't have wide scope, then the statement made there would be false, i.e. somebody could comment with (68), which is good in some sense, since the person uttering it may have taken (67)a in the narrow scope reading.

(68) No, you don't know that.

Here again speaker A may reply with (69), making clear that speaker B assigned the wrong reading to (67)c.

(69) Oh! You misunderstood me.

More evidence comes from the fact that speaker B may continue (67)c with (70):

(70) Now that you know who remembers where we bought which book, I hope you won't go everywhere repeating it.

Again, it is not clear that those readings can be explained in Kuno and Robinson's analysis.

This ends my arguments in favor of the ambiguous analysis of iterative questions like (1). I will now turn to examples like (10) and to some problems.

(10) Who knows where we bought these books?

5.3 Definite NP's and some problems

As we have seen in 5.1, Kuno and Robinson took the fact that sentences like (10) allowed answers like (5) as an indication that it was not necessary to assume that *which book* had to be bound by the same Q-marker that bounded *who* to explain why (5) was apparently a good answer to (1), since non wh-phrases can't be bound by Q-markers.

(10) Who knows where Mary bought these books?

(5) Peter knows where Mary bought *Aspects* and Paul knows where Mary bought *Syntactic Structures*, and Fred knows where Mary bought *Structural Linguistics*.

(1) Who knows where Mary bought which book?

They didn't take into consideration the possibility that *these books* could perhaps take widest scope in (10) just as we have agreed that *every student* could take widest scope in (71):

(71) What grade does every student deserve?

That is, it is possible that (10) has a reading similar to that of (72):

(72) For these books, I ask you to tell me who knows where we bought them.

If *these books* can have such a scope, it is still not sure that we would expect answers like (5): it all depends on whether or not *these books* can have an individual, a distributive reading (just as *each of these books*) in addition to a group reading, as argued by M. Bennett (1974). Sentences like the following one suggest that it can.

(73) Peter knows where Malone killed the poor victims.

It seems clear that one of the ways that this sentence can be understood is similar to (74):

(74) For each of the poor victims, Peter knows where the murderer killed it.

One way to explain this is to assume that definite NP's in the plural can have a distributive reading. If this is so, (10) could be represented by (75) in the Montague framework; a_p is a sorted variable ranging over place adverbials.

(75) $\Lambda y [\text{book}'(y) \rightarrow ?\lambda P^{\vee} P(\hat{x}_o [\text{person}'(x_o) \ \& \ \text{know}'(x_o, \hat{\ }\lambda a_p [a_p (\hat{\ }\text{buy}'_{*} (m, \check{\ }y))])])] \ \& \ \forall y \ \text{book}'\{y\}_{\geq 2}$

Let us look now at some possible evidence that *these books* can have widest scope in (10).

Consider the following sentence:

(76) Who knows where we bought these books and who already did yesterday?

It seems that here, where we have an empty VP, only a non-multiple answer is possible:

(77) John knows where we bought these books and Mary already did yesterday.

One can check that if *these books* is given widest scope in (76), then after VP copying occurs there will be an unbound variable in the second conjunct. This will not be the case if *these books* is assigned narrow scope.[8] The difference in possible answers to (10) and (76) can be taken as evidence that in (10) *these books* can have widest scope, while in (76) it cannot.

There is a problem however, We expect sentences like (79) parallel to (78) ((37) above) but with *these books* rather than *which book*, to allow answers like (80) ((39) above), since sentences like (1) and (10) both allow answers like (5); but in fact (80) is not an appropriate answer to (79).

(78) Which girl discovered where we bought which book before which boy did?

(79) Which girl discovered where we bought these books before which boy did?

(80) Mary discovered where we bought *Syntactic Structures* before Alan did, and Sue discovered where we bought *Aspects* before Fred did.

How can these facts be explained? Notice that in (78)-(79) we have *which girl* while in (1) and (10) we have *who*. If we replace *who* by *which girl* in (10) which gives us (81), a multiple answer such as (5) is no longer possible:

(81) Which girl knows where we bought these books?

One thing that this may suggest is that after all *these books* doesn't really have a distributive reading, contrary to what we assumed was the case when we discussed (10). Assuming on the basis of the different sorts of answers possible to (10) and (76) that *these books* in (10) and (79) can have widest scope, the problem is to explain why a multiple reply to (10) is possible. Part of the answer must be related to the fact that *who* in a question allows for values in the singular or the plural in the answer, while *which girl* for example, allows only for values in the singular. So, (82)a can be answered with (83)a and b while (82)b only allows answers like (83)a:

(82) a. Who came?

　　　b. Which girl came?

(83) a. Mary came.

　　　b. Mary and Sue came.

Looking at (84), which differs from (10) in that it is clear here that *the watch* doesn't have a distributive reading, seems to support the hypothesis that the crucial factor in (10) and (79) doesn't have much to do with a possible distributive reading of *these books*.

(84) Who remembers how to put the watch together?

(85)a,b, and c are possible answers to (84); many speakers consider however that (85)b can be given as an answer only when no answer like (85)a exists, given the facts or their knowledge of them. (85)b can somehow be considered as short for (85)c:[9]

(85) a. Peter does.

　　　b. Peter remembers how to do the escapement, and Mary can handle the drive mechanisms, and John is good with the discs.

　　　c. Nobody completely, but Peter remembers how to do the escapement, and Mary can handle the drive mechanisms, and John is good with the discs.

What is interesting is that a question like (86)a, with a missing VP, doesn't allow a multiple answer, i.e. answers like (86)b are appropriate, but answers like (86)c are not.

(86) a. Who remembers how to put the watch together and who will very soon?

b. Peter, Paul, and Mary do, and Fred and Sue will very soon.

c. Peter knows how to do the escapement, and Fred will very soon, and Mary can handle the drive mechanisms, and Sue will very soon,....

This suggests that even though *the watch* in (84) doesn't have a distributive reading, scope possibilities are crucial in accounting for why (84) can receive a multiple answer and (86)a not. In addition, as the answer to (84) shows, the person who answers takes advantage of the fact that a watch is made of different parts to give a helpful answer. We face however the same problem that we did with (10). If we replace *who* by *which person* in (84), so as to get (87), a multiple answer seems to be inappropriate:

(87) Which person knows how to put the watch together?

The difference between *who* and *which person* is thus important. It is as if *who* was standing for a group, a team. We can thus think of (84) as equivalent to (88):

(88) Which people (together) know how to put the watch together?

(89) would be a direct answer, but (85)b could be considered as a more detailed and helpful answer.

(89) Peter, Mary, and John together know.

This sort of reasoning could be extended to (10).

To summarize, it seems that two elements are crucial.

1) Scope possibilities play a role, as the contrast between the possible answers to (10) and (76) as well as between (84) and (86)a shows.

2) The difference between the possible answers to (10) and (81), (84) and (87) shows that the fact that *who* can stand for a group while *which person* for example cannot is crucial. In fact, it seems that if we replace *who* by *which persons* in (10), a multiple answer is also inappropriate. This is probably due to the fact that with *which persons* each individual must have the relevant property.

5.4 Iterative questions and *whether*

One of the consequences of letting *what* in (90) have narrow or wide scope is that it predicts that sentences like (91) should be grammatical when *what* takes widest scope. We postpone judgments (indicating that with the symbol 'o').

(90) Who knows where we bought what?

(91) Who wonders whether who came?

In the framework used in this chapter, (91) can be represented as in (92)a; it is represented as (92)b in the framework discussed in the first two chapters and as (92)c in Karttunen's framework.

(92) a. [who$_1$ [who$_2$[t$_2$ knows [whether [t$_1$ came]]]]]
$\bar{S}$ $\bar{S}$ S $\bar{S}$ S

b. ?$^\wedge\lambda P_1 \lambda P_2 [P_2 (^\wedge\text{know}'(^\wedge\lambda q\ q(\ P_1 (^\wedge\text{came}'))))]$

c. ?$(\hat{p}\ Vx\ Vy\ [^vp\ \&\ [p=^\wedge\text{know}'(y,\ \hat{q}\ [^vq\ \&\ q=^\wedge\text{came}^!_*(^vx)$

$\vee\ q=^\wedge\text{-came}^!_*(^vx)])]])$

(93) would be an appropriate answer to a question like (1) analyzed as in (92).

(93) Peter knows whether Mary came and Fred knows whether Sue came.

Questions like (91) are however generally considered as ungrammatical and in fact Kuno and Robinson (1972:473) have taken the supposed ungrammaticality of (91) as an argument for saying that there the unmoved wh-phrase under *whether* can't take widest scope and that this confirms their theory that in (90), *what* must have scope over the same sentence as *where*. A few examples from the literature, with the original judgments follow:

(94) a. *Tell me who is not sure if he should read which books.

b. *Tell me who wants to know if he should buy what.

c. *Who asked if he could see who is not known.

d. *Who remembers whether John kissed who?

(94)a-c come from Kuno and Robinson (1972:473) and (94)d from Hankamer (1974:71). Hankamer provides the same judgment on a Turkish equivalent of (94)d.

Some people however have different judgments. Hull (1974:473) disagrees with Kuno and Robinson and reports that his informants consider (94)c as grammatical. It is impossible to tell from his work whether the judgments he reports on (94)c extend to the other examples of that kind. I have also found a few speakers, a small minority, who consider many, though not all, examples of that kind as grammatical. My judgments on similar French examples vary from example to example. They seem more acceptable in contexts in which the value for each wh-phrase is known in advance, but the correct pairings are not. It has already been pointed out that this sort of situation was the best one for multiple questions, at first sight at least; see for example Hankamer (1974:73, fn. 3). In such contexts, I don't find the examples in (95) bad at all, interpreted as genuine questions, i.e. not as echo-questions or quiz-questions.

(95) a. Qui sait si qui va venir?

Who knows whether who will come?

b. Qui t'a dit si qui allait venir?

Who told you whether who was going to come?

c. Qui sait si quel travail est fini?

Who knows whether what work is done?

The judgments may however be influenced by the analysis I defend. Let us assume for the sake of discussion that such examples are in fact ungrammatical; does this really provide strong evidence against the correctness of the claim that examples such as (1) are ambiguous? Given the vast amount of evidence we have provided in favor of the claim that (1) was ambiguous, we are led to say that if examples such as (94) and (95) are ungrammatical, it is not because unmoved wh-phrases must always have narrowest scope, but because of some independent reason. An indication that such an independent reason may indeed exist comes from considering examples such as in (96), with *that* instead of *whether*; the examples come from Kuno and Robinson (1972:465-467):

(96) a. *Tell me who remembers that we bought these books where.

b. *Tell me who predicted that John would come when.

c. *Tell me who arranged for who to come.

d. *Tell me who persuaded Mary that John likes who.

They proposed the Clause Mate Constraint on Multiple WH words (1972:471) to account for such facts:

> Multiple wh words bound by the same Q must be clause mates at the time of application of WH-Q movement.

This correctly predicts the ungrammaticality of (94) and (96), as well as the grammaticality of examples such as (97), where the fronted wh-phrase was the clause-mate of the unmoved wh-phrase before wh-movement applied.

(97) a. Tell me who John thinks killed who.

b. What do you expect Mary will do to who?

Hankamer (1974:65) agrees with most of the judgments Kuno and Robinson give for their examples -- though not with all the judgments -- but he also brings up many examples like (98) and (13, above) that contradict the prediction of their constraint:

(98) a. Tell me who claimed that Sue was kissing who.

b. Who thinks that we should send this stuff where?

Kuno and Robinson's constraint is thus too strong for such examples, just as it was too strong for the iterative questions like (1). An interesting observation made by Hankamer is that the worst examples like (96) are found when the embedded unmoved wh-phrase is in a factive complement. One possibility is that the examples in (94) are ungrammatical for a reason similar to why the examples in (96) are. More work is still necessary before anything sure can be said about examples of the type of (94), (95), and (96).

Let us now turn to Hankamer's account of why examples like (94) should be ungrammatical. Hankamer claims that the indexing theory derived from Baker's work predicts the ungrammaticality of examples like (94). In Hankamer (1974) this theory has the following features: a wh-phrase and a Q-clause are coindexed; a Q-clause is a clause which is interpreted as a question (excluding concealed questions). Hankamer then says (1974:69):

> The indexing theory makes a further prediction, based on the fact that any Q clause which contains one or more WH words must have at least one wh-word indexed to it. Thus we have no examples like *who remembers whether Charley shot who? where both WH words are indexed to the root clause, and no WH is indexed to the embedded Q clause.

As far as I understand the indexing theory, it only says that each wh-phrase must be indexed to some Q-clause. But since Hankamer doesn't consider that the *whether* or the *if* of examples like (91), (93), (94) are coindexed with the Q-clauses that they are heading, the indexing theory doesn't require that each Q-clause must have a wh-phrase indexed to it; if it is the case that a Q-clause containing a wh-phrase must have a wh-phrase indexed to it, it must be because of some reason which does not follow automatically from the indexing theory. Notice also that if *whether* or *if* is considered as coindexed with the Q-clause that they are heading, which would be the normal way to reinterpret in Hankamer's informal analysis, the analysis of *whether*-clauses discussed in chapter II and that proposed by Karttunen (1977a,b), then in cases like (94) the unmoved wh-phrase should be able to have widest scope. What we can do at this point is examine another variant of questions with *whether* and see whether the predictions Hankamer says the indexing theory make in the case of examples like (94) also hold for this other type of example or not. In the case the predictions are incorrect, Hankamer's explanation for (94) should be abandoned. The relevant type of example is exemplified in (99); I consider both English and French examples.

(99) a. Who knows whether the butler revealed who ate what?

b. Qui sait si Pierre a révélé à l'ennemi qui leur a volé quel document?

Who knows whether Peter revealed to the enemy who stole what document from them.

These examples have the following structure:

(100) a. $[wh_1 \ldots [\text{whether} \ldots [wh_2 \ldots wh_3 \ldots]]]$

$\overline{S}_1 \quad\quad\quad \overline{S}_2 \quad\quad\quad \overline{S}_3$

Can wh_3 have widest scope? If it can, then a wh-word inside a *whether*-clause may have scope wider than that clause; i.e. the wh-word in a *whether*-clause can be indexed to a clause containing the *whether*-clause. I have clearly the intuition that (101) is a possible answer to (99)b. This is the sort of answer that is predicted if *quel document* in (99)b can be interpreted with widest scope.

(101) Le directeur de la marine sait si Pierre a révélé à l'ennemi qui leur a volé les plans des sous-marins, et le directeur de l'aviation sait si Pierre a révélé à l'ennemi qui leur a volé les plans de leur système d'alerte, etc.

(101) continued...

The Head of the Navy knows whether Peter revealed to the enemy who stole the submarine plans from them, and the Head of the Air Force knows whether Peter revealed to the enemy who stole the plans of their alert system, etc.

We can also test whether wh_3 in (100) can have widest scope by using the sorts of facts we examined when we argued that sentences like (1) were ambiguous:

(1) Who knows where Mary bought which book?

Consider for example (102), where the square brackets indicate that the two most deeply embedded questions are coordinated:

(102) Who knows whether Peter told the Director [which boy subscribed to which magazine and which girl did too]?

Although speakers have at first difficulty to report clear judgments on such a sentence, they finally tend to find it good; they have no doubt however that (103)a and (103)b are ungrammatical:

(103) a. *Which boy subscribed to which magazine and which girl did too?

b. *Fred knows whether Peter told the Director which boy subscribed to which magazine and which girl did too.

Since the only difference between (102) and (103)a lies in the alternation between *who* and *Fred*, I take the fact that (102) tends to be accepted while (103)b is not as indicating that *which magazine* in (102) has widest scope; that is, the logical form of (102), after VP-copying, is (104), where all variables are properly bound; in particular, *which magazine*$_1$ c-commands all occurences of t_1.

(104) [which magazine$_1$ [who$_2$ [t_2 knows [whether Peter told the Director [[which boy$_3$ [t_3 subscribed to t_1]] and [which girl$_4$ [t_4 subscribed to t_1 too]]]]]]]

The claim that wh_3 in (100) can have widest scope is supported by examples like (105), which I accept; the English version is also accepted:

(105) Qui sait si Pierre a oublié comment interpréter laquelle de ces formules?

Who knows whether Peter has forgotten how to interpret which of these formulas?

If *qui* or *who* are replaced by a non-wh-phrase, preventing thus the most deeply embedded wh-phrase to have widest scope, the result is ungrammatical. The grammaticality of (105) is explained if we assume that the unmoved wh-phrase can have widest scope.

I conclude this chapter very briefly:

1) Questions like (1) are ambiguous.

2) This has been shown in 5.2.1 to 5.2.4.

3) In structures like (100), the most deeply embedded wh-phrase, wh_3, can have widest scope, i.e. *whether* doesn't prevent the existence of this scope assignment. Consequently, in cases like (91), (94), (96), in 5.4, the introducer of the yes-no question (*whether/ if/ si*) should not automatically prevent the unmoved wh-phrase to have widest scope. If it doesn't have widest scope, it is for an as yet to be discovered reason.

FOOTNOTES TO CHAPTER V

1. I have followed Karttunen (1977a:28) in assuming for convenience that *where* was a noun phrase rather than an adverbial phrase. If we were to use Karttunen's analysis, it would be more convenient too to not make use of the 'Relation Notation' (PTQ, 259), i.e. to use representation as in (i)a and (i)b:

(i) a. $\hat{p}$ Vz[$^{\vee}$p & p= $\hat{P}$P{z}($^{\wedge}$know'($\hat{q}$ Vy Vx[book'(y)

 & place'(x) &$^{\vee}$q & q=

 $^{\wedge}$m*($^{\wedge}$(at'($\hat{P}$P{y})) ($^{\wedge}$buy'($\hat{P}$P{x})))])]

b. $\hat{p}$ Vy Vz[book'(x) & $^{\vee}$p & p= $\hat{P}$P{z}($^{\wedge}$know'($\hat{q}$ Vx [place'(x)

 & $^{\vee}$q & q=

 $^{\wedge}$m*($^{\wedge}$(at'($\hat{P}$P{x})) ($^{\wedge}$buy'($\hat{P}$P{y})))])]

2. (9) is not exactly the representation that Kuno and Robinson give. We add the distinction between $\bar{S}$ and S. The Q marker is similar to Chomsky's +wh marker for direct and indirect interrogatives. For arguments that interpretation is done after application of wh-movement, i.e. deep structure is not enough, see Hankamer (1974).

3. Note that *which boy$_4$* is unmoved, as evidenced by the fact that in those types of sentences a questioned object is unmoved:

(i) *I wonder which girl left before which boy Fred talked to.

 I wonder which girl left before Fred talked to which boy.

(ii) *I wonder which girl John talked to before which boy Fred talked to.

 I wonder which girl John talked to before Fred talked to which boy.

(iii) I wonder who talked to which girl before Fred talked to which boy.

4. Things seem to be different in French in cases like:

(i)   Je me demande qui est-ce qui a épousé qui.
      I wonder who married who.

But it seems more difficult in cases like (ii) with stress on *c'est*:

(ii) Je me demande qui c'est qui a épousé qui.
      I wonder who it is that married who.

(i) seems bad also when there is rising intonation on *est-ce*. *Qui est-ce qui* in (i) may have two analyses. When it is a real cleft it is ungrammatical. When *qui est-ce qui* is reanalyzed as a unit, along the lines of Obenauer (1977), as equivalent to *qui*, (i) is grammatical, since we don't have a cleft in fact. I often find it difficult to have clear judgments on the French data and won't discuss them.

5. (55), along with (i), was given to us by B. H. Partee, as an example where the person who asks the question knows the answer to the embedded question and doesn't want an answer to this embedded question in the end:

(i)   Who told the police where we hid which documents?

(i.e., the speaker in this particular occasion may be only interested in the answer to the question under its wide scope reading),

6. Intuitively, what seems wrong to me with (56)c is that the question is equivalent to asking how one interprets a subset of the formulas, but which subset is relevant is not indicated. As far as I can tell, we have the same sort of data when we made the scope more explicit:

(i)   a. For which of these formulas, who has forgotten how
         we interpret it?

      b. *For which of these formulas, how do we interpret it?

It seems that we might possibly find the same sort of restriction with ordinary quantifiers:

(ii) a. Who has forgotten how we interpret one of these formulas?

      b. ?How do we interpret one of these formulas?

7. The same observation can be made if we replace *who* by *which one of these students*:

(i) Which one of these students has forgotten how to interpret which of these formulas?

(ii) Which one of these students has forgotten which of these formulas?

8. In the system we have defended in Chapter II, with a performative analysis, we are obliged to have a performative with each question, otherwise in cases like (76) all traces will be properly bound. Compare:

(i) [these books$_i$ [?who knows where we bought t$_i$ and

who already did [know where we bought t$_i$] yesterday]]

(ii) [[these books$_i$ [?who knows where we bought t$_i$]] and

[?who already did [know where we bought t$_i$] yesterday]]

In (i) the second occurence of t$_i$ is c-commanded by *these books* but it is not in (ii).

9. I owe (84)-(85) to Roger Higgins.

CHAPTER VI

THE ALTERNATION BETWEEN *QUOI* AND *QUE* IN QUESTIONS IN FRENCH

6.0 Introduction

Kayne (1974) has given a lot of evidence that *que* in (1)a is not a relative pronoun, and that *qui* in (1)b isn't either, contrary to what was assumed until then by most traditional and transformational grammarians.[1]

(1) a. La table QUE tu vois est belle.

The table that you see is pretty.

b. La table QUI se trouve dans le coin est belle.

The table that sits in the corner is pretty.

He claims that *que* and *qui* in restrictive relative clauses, when they are not the complement of a preposition, are the complementizers *que* and *qui* that also introduce the subordinate clauses in (2)a and (2)b. The claim that *qui* in (2)b is a complementizer had already been made by Gross (1968) and Moreau (1970, 1971).

(2) a. Je crois QUE Pierre est malade.

I believe that Peter is ill.

b. Qui veux-tu QUI vienne?

Who do you want to come?

It is thus claimed that in surface structure the relative clauses in (1) don't contain any relative pronoun. French is in this respect like many other languages which can construct some or all of their relative clauses without a relative pronoun on the surface: Yiddish is of the first type, as Lowenstamm (1977) has shown, and English is of the second type. Not only may English lack a relative pronoun but it may even lack the complementizer.

(3) a. The man that you met is here.

b. The man you met is here.

That *that* in (3)a is not a relative pronoun but the conjunction (the complementizer in today's terminology), can be found in Jespersen (MEG:III), Klima (1964), and after that in most of the recent transformational literature.

Obenauer (1976, 1977) argues that likewise the *que* that is found in direct questions like (4)a-c is the complementizer rather than an interrogative pronoun for inanimates, as had always been assumed.

(4) a. QUE veux-tu?

What do you want?

b. QUE va-t-il devenir?

What will he become?

c. QUE crains-tu qui se passe?

What are you afraid will happen?

To my knowledge, French is the first language for which it is claimed that some wh-questions don't have a wh-word in surface structure (I put aside here concealed questions). I will argue that French isn't so surprisingly different from what has been assumed and that *que* in questions like (4) is an interrogative pronoun. The discussion of the alternation between *que* and *quoi* in questions will be useful in the chapter on free relatives too.

6.1 Background

6.1.1

In this discussion I will assume that the categorial component of the grammar of French contains the following two rules:

(5) a. $\bar{S} \rightarrow$ Comp S

b. Comp → complementizer

The choice of the correct lexical item as complementizer will be made between *que* and *qui*, which we assume to be allomorphs of the same morpheme, which we will represent by QUE, and *si* (for yes/no questions), à, *de*, ∅ for infinitival complements. I don't adopt Chomsky's features ±WH. Grimshaw (1977) showed that those features play no role in subcategorization and that for example the distribution of *that* and *whether* in Middle English, where they cooccur, can't be accounted for by them. They play no role in French in the choice of complementizer as far as I can see. I assume that the choice of complementizer is made in part on the basis of whether the following sentence is in a finite tense or not: *QUE* or *si* are chosen in front of a tensed clause, the other complementizers in front of a non-tensed clause, if à and *de* are really complementizers. For most of our discussion it only matters that *QUE* is a complementizer for tensed clauses (Kayne,

1974:60). For our purpose it doesn't matter how early the choice
of the complementizer is done, as long as it occurs before the
application of a certain number of rules that we will present right
now.

6.1.2 French relative clauses and the que/qui complementizers

We give here only what is going to be useful for the discussion
of questions. To account for the distribution of the complementizer
que and *qui* in relative clauses like (6)a-d, four rules are necessary.
They are given in (7).

(6) a. Le garçon QUI est venu
        The boy that came

    b. Le garçon QUE tu vois
        The boy that you see

    c. Le garçon QUE tu voulais qui vienne
        The boy that you wanted to come

    d. Le garçon QUE tu voulais que je rencontre
        The boy that you wanted me to meet

    e. Le garçon avec lequel tu voulais que je parle
        The boy with whom you wanted me to speak

(7) a. Complementizer insertion. I will assume that the
        insertion of *que* is done in deep structure. The
        only important thing is that it occurs before Rel
        NP deletion, presented in (7)c.

    b. Wh-movement: moves NP's, PP's, and AdvP's which
        contain a wh-phrase into COMP.

    c. Relative NP deletion. This rule deletes NP's
        immediately dominated by Comp. It is formulated
        as (i) by Kayne, where -WH stands for *QUE* in fact.

        (i) [NP [NP -WH] X] → 1 Ø 3 4
                Comp
             1   2   3   4

        Kayne (1975:48-49) assumes that QUE is already present
        at the moment of application of rule (i).

(7) d. *Que-deletion*. This rule deletes the complementizer when it cooccurs in Comp with another phrase:

(ii) [W que] → 1 ∅
      Comp
       1 2

where W is non-null

e. *Que/qui alternation*. The complementizer is *qui* when the subject of the clause that it heads has been removed from its clause by a movement rule or a deletion rule, and *que* in the other cases. Many analyses of this are possible. Assuming that the rule of Stylistic Inversion (Kayne, 1972), which moves a subject within its own clause, doesn't leave a trace (Chomsky, 1977) the que/qui alternation can be described as follows:

(iii) a. QUE → qui / [───────] [e]
                     Comp NP_i

b. QUE → que

I assume that (iii)b applies after (iii)a. Here QUE is an abbreviation for a set of universal features (Chomsky, 1977: fn. 53). Other analyses of the que/qui alternation are possible (see Kayne 1976, 1975a and Kayne and Pollock (1978)).

We will go through the derivation of examples (6)c and (6)e to show how these rules work. The derivations are grossly simplified.

Let us assume that (9)a is the simplified deep structure of (6)c; the choice between *qui* and *lequel* as relative pronoun is immaterial here.

(9) a. [[le garçon] [[QUE] [tu voulais [[QUE]
                          Comp
    NP NP_i $\bar{S}$ $\bar{S}$ Comp

       [[{lequel}] vienne]]]]]
          {qui   }
        $\bar{S}$ NP_i

(9)b is derived by application of WH-movement:

    b. Le garçon$_i$ [[[{lequel / qui}] QUE] tu voulais QUE
                                                NP$_i$
                    $\overline{S}$ Comp

            [e]   vienne]]
            NP$_i$

Rel NP deletion removes the wh-NP phrase from the Comp in which it is; the result is (9)c:

    c. Le garçon$_i$ [[QUE] tu voulais QUE [e] vienne
                                                          NP$_i$

Each occurrence of QUE is then realized in the appropriate way according to rules (iii)a and (iii)b:

    d. Le garçon *que* tu voulais *qui* vienne

In the case of (6)e, we will assume the deep structure (10)a. Application of wh-movement gives (10)b; at that point Rel NP deletion is inapplicable. Que-deletion can apply, changing (10)b into (10)c. (10)d is finally derived by application of (iii)b.

    (10) a. Le garçon$_i$ [[QUE] tu voulais [[QUE] je parle avec
                          $\overline{S}$ Comp $\overline{S}$ Comp

        [lequel]]]
        NP$_i$

        b. Le garçon [[[avec lequel] QUE] tu voulais QUE
                        $\overline{S}$ Comp   PP$_i$

      je parle [e]]
              PP$_i$

        c. Le garçon [[[avec lequel]] tu voulais QUE
                        $\overline{S}$ Comp   PP$_i$

      je parle [e]]
              PP$_i$

        d. Le garçon *avec lequel* tu voulais *que* je parle

With this background we can turn to questions. We will first restrict ourselves to tensed clauses and then to infinitival clauses.

6.2 Tensed clauses

6.2.1 Distribution of *quoi* and *que*

The statements about the distribution of *quoi* and *que* are easier to make if we may make reference to the COMP position, i.e. we must distinguish between those wh-phrases that are in Comp position as the result of the application of wh-movement and those that are not, as with unmoved wh-phrases.

Taking *qui* to illustrate when we consider that a wh-phrase is in Comp, consider the following examples:

(11) a. QUI veux-tu que je rencontre?

b. QUI veux que QUI vienne?

c. Tu as vu QUI?

d. QUI est venu?

In (11)a, *qui* has been moved and is in Comp. In (11)c, *qui* is unmoved and not in Comp. (11)d can be analyzed in two ways. Wh-movement may have applied, in which case *qui* is in Comp. But it may also be a case without wh-movement parallel to (11)c or (11)e:

e. Tu crois que QUI est venu?

In (11)b, the first occurence of *qui* is in Comp or not, just as was the case for *qui* in (11)d. The second occurence of *qui* is not in Comp.

In the case of indirect question, wh-movement is obligatory and a sentence initial wh-phrase is always in Comp.

Let us turn to *que* and *quoi*. We consider direct questions first. When the wh-phrase is not in Comp, *quoi* is required.

(12) a. Tu as acheté QUOI?

b. Qui pense à QUOI?

c. Qui croit que QUOI va arriver?

If the wh-phrase is moved in Comp, we must distinguish among several cases. If the word is the complement of a preposition, *quoi* is used:

(13) a. A quoi penses-tu?

b. *A que penses-tu?

What are you thinking about?

If the wh-word is not the complement of a preposition and occurs alone in Comp, *que* must be used (with one restriction to which we will come immediately).

(14) a. *Quoi veux-tu acheter?

b. Que veux-tu acheter?

What do you want to buy?

(15) a. *Quoi penses-tu qui se soit passé?

b. Que penses-tu qui se soit passé?

What do you think happened?

If however the questioned wh-phrase is the subject of the main clause, neither *que* nor *quoi* are good.

(16) a. *Quoi s'est passé?

b. *Que s'est passé?

A more general characterization of this case is to say that neither *que* nor *quoi* are good when they are adjacent to the position from which they were extracted.

We have looked at (16)a assuming the wh-phrase to be in Comp. Examples similar to (16)a are sometimes mentioned as grammatical, for example in Moignet (1974:175):

La fonction de sujet peut se recontrer en parlure familiere:

Quoi t'a étonné?

Les exemples de ce type sont rares, mais on en trouve comme variante de *quoi?* en phrase elliptique.

Quelque chose m'a étonné.-*Quoi* t'a étonné?

(The subject function may be found in colloquial speech;

WHAT surprised you?

Examples of that type are rare, but may be found as a variant of *what?* in elliptical sentences:

Something surprised me. -WHAT surprised you?)

Obenauer (1976:93, fn. 18) mentions these cases, and correctly points out that in such examples *quoi* is stressed and the interpretation is that of echo-questions. Further support to the claim that in such examples *quoi* is not in COMP comes from indirect questions; in indirect questions, where wh-movement must apply, the examples parallel to (16)a are always ungrammatical:

(17) *Je me demande quoi s'est passé.
I wonder what happened.

Let us also mention that sentences like (18), with *qui* for inanimates on the model of what we found in headed restrictive relatives, are ungrammatical:

(18) *Qui s'est passé?

Instead of (16), or (18), (19) must be used:

(19) Qu'est-ce qui s'est passé?

Finally, if the wh-phrase is not the complement of a preposition but the wh-phrase is modified by *d'autre* (else) or *de+Adj* (of+Adj), or is coordinated to another wh-phrase, *quoi* can be used.

(20) a. Quoi d'autre veux-tu acheter?
What else do you want to buy?

b. Quoi de neuf as-tu a m'apprendre?
What do you have to tell me that is new?

c. Quoi d'autre pourrait m'amener chez toi?
What else could bring me to your place? (Obenauer, 1977:28, from Sandfeld, 1928:320)

d. Quoi de neuf a-t-on annoncé?
What that is new has been announced?

(20) e. Qui ou quoi vous a donné cette idée?

Who or what gave you that idea? (Obenauer, 1977:28, fn. 32, from Sandfeld, 1928:320)

Que can never be used here, except perhaps in the last case, i.e. in examples like (21). As most people reject them, I will assume they are ungrammatical:

(21) a. ?? Qui ou que voulez-vous photographier?

b. Who or what do you want to take pictures of?

c. *Que ou qui voulez-vous photographier?

We can quickly run through indirect questions now.

First of all, all the embedded equivalents of the direct questions with *quoi* have the same quality as the direct questions:

(22) a. *Je me demande QUOI tu veux acheter.

I wonder what you want to buy.

b. Je me demande quoi D'AUTRE tu veux acheter.

I wonder what else you want to buy.

All the examples where *que* was grammatical or ungrammatical in direct questions are ungrammatical when embedded:

(23) a. *Je me demande QUE tu veux acheter.

I wonder what you want to buy.

b. *Je me demande QUE se passe.

I wonder what is happening.

Instead one must use *ce que* where *que* was grammatical and *ce qui* where *qu'est-ce qui* was used. In many varieties of French one can also use *qu'est-ce que* and *qu'est-ce qui*:

(24) a. Je me demande CE QUE tu veux acheter.

Je me demande QU'EST-CE que tu veux acheter.

I wonder what you want to buy.

(25) a. Je me demande CE QUI se passe.

b. Je me demande QU'EST-CE QUI se passe.

I wonder what is happening.

The *a* cases are probably relative clauses with concealed question interpretation. The *b* examples have been discussed in the transformational literature by, among others, Langacker (1965, 1972), Hirschbühler (1970), Huddleston and Uren (1969), and most recently by Obenauer (1976, 1977). These constructions won't be discussed here.

This represents the basic data. Other facts will be introduced in time.

6.2.2 The traditional view.

The traditional view is that in questions, both *quoi* and *que* are interrogative pronouns; see for example Grevisse (1964, 569 sqq), Gougenheim (1970:108-112), and in the transformational framework Langacker (1965, 1972). Since *quoi* and *que* are in complementary distribution, it is possible to look at them as morphological variants of the same morpheme. Taking *quoi* as basic, we will formalize the traditional view by means of rule (26).

(26) [quoi] → [que]
                COMP

We turn now to Obenauer's analysis.

6.2.3 Obenauer's analysis.

Obenauer (1976, 1977) argues that *que* in (27) is not an interrogative pronoun but the complementizer.

(27) Que fait Pierre?
      What is Peter doing?

His analysis can be summarized as follows:

a) every tensed sentence in French is introduced by the complementizer *que* at some point in the derivation. His analysis is compatible with the hypothesis that the complementizer is present in deep structure (see Obenauer, 1976:123-124). We adopt that hypothesis. The essential aspects of the deep structure of (27) can then be represented by (28) (see Obenauer, 1976:124).

(28) [[que] Pierre fait QUOI]
       S̄ Comp

b) Wh-movement moves *quoi* in Comp to the left of *que*:

(29) [[quoi que] Pierre fait

c) Stylistic Inversion (Kayne, 1972) moves the subject at the end of the clause.

d) At this point, a rule deleting *quoi* in Comp is applied. The rule is formulated by Obenauer (1977:321) as in (30) though the variable X should be omitted, at least to account for examples like (20)a-d (see Obenauer, 1977:324, fn. 32):

(30) PAS-DE-QUOI

[quoi X que] → ∅ 2
Comp
   1   2

Application of Stylistic Inversion and Pas-de-quoi to (29) gives (31):

(31) [[que] fait Pierre?]
     S̄ Comp

The derivation of sentences like (27) can be contrasted with the derivation of sentences like (32):

(32) De quoi parle Pierre?

About what is Pierre talking?

After application of wh-movement and Stylistic Inversion, the underlying structure of (32) is as in (33):

(33) [[de quoi que] parle Pierre]

At this point, Pas-de-quoi is inapplicable. *Que* is then deleted by Kayne's Que-deletion rule (see (7)d above), ordered after Pas-de-quoi:

(34) [[de quoi] parle Pierre?]
     S̄ Comp

This represents the core of Obenauer's analysis. In the next section his arguments against the traditional analysis and in favor of his will be presented and examined. Additional facts will be discussed.

6.2.4 Obenauer's arguments.

6.2.4.1 Indirect questions.

Both analyses predict the ungrammaticality of sentences like (35)a, but not of (35)b:

(35) a. *Je me demande QUOI tu as vu là-bas.

   b. *Je me demande QUE tu as vu là-bas.
      I wonder what you saw there.

Under the hypothesis that *que* is a pronoun, (35)b should be excluded by a constraint saying that the *que* pronoun may not introduce a subordinate clause. The formulation given is (1977:314):

(36) The object form *que* of the pronoun *quoi* may not head an embedded sentence.

This analysis would also account for the ungrammaticality of free relatives like (37), assuming that the wh-phrase is in Comp position (see Obenauer, 1977:314 and chapter VII here).

(37) a. *J'ai acheté QUOI tu as acheté.

   b. *J'ai acheté QUE tu as acheté.
      I bought what you bought.

Obenauer attacks the pronominal view on the grounds that it is mysterious why a pronominal form would lead to opposite grammaticality status in main and embedded clauses. Moreover, he claims that something like (36) doesn't account for another case, exclamative clauses, where *que* is ungrammatical in embedded clauses, but not in main clauses, though it is clearly not an allomorph of *quoi*, it is not a pronoun:

(38) a. Que vous avez de préjugés!
      How much prejudice you have!

   b. *C'est ahurissant que vous avez de préjugés!
      It's amazing how much prejudice you have!

The traditional analysis of *que* in (38)a considers it as a QUANTIFIER. Thus, Obenauer concludes (1977:314), (36) would have to be supplemented by an additional constraint to take care of exclamative clauses:

(39) Exclamative *que* may not head an embedded sentence.

According to him, not only are (36) and (39) ad hoc by themselves, but this approach apparently misses a generalization that could be captured if the *que*'s in indirect questions, free relatives, and exclamatives were the same element.[2] Obenauer proposes the following account. The *que*'s in direct and indirect questions, direct and indirect exclamatives, and free relatives are just instances of the complementizer. If this is the case, then (35)b, (37)b, and (38)b can be excluded by the following condition (Obenauer, 1977:326):

(40) In a structure of the form [... [[que] ...] ...]
                                  $\bar{S}$ $\bar{S}$ Comp

   where there is no possible antecedent for *que*, the interpretation can only be that of neutral embedding.

This means that if the *que*-clause is not a relative clause with an overt antecedent, the only interpretation that will be allowed is that of a complement clause. Since Obenauer said that if *que* here was a pronoun we would not expect a difference between main and subordinate clauses, I assume that Obenauer thinks that a constraint like (40) is most natural if *que* is a complementizer.

We will now discuss several points made by Obenauer and see that the traditional approach should be maintained.

Let us take (40) first. Notice that even assuming that *que* is a pronoun in (35)b and (37)b, and that it is a quantifier in (38)b, the constraint (40) will still exclude these examples, since the only thing that it requires is that there be a *que* in the Comp of an embedded clause. Another point is that assuming that the *que*'s which lead to ungrammaticality in indirect questions, indirect exclamatives, and free relatives are not complementizers, we could replace (40) by (41), which doesn't make reference to semantic interpretation:

(41) A structure of the form [...[que...]...] is marked
                                S $\bar{S}$

   as ungrammatical, unless *que* is a complementizer.

We will see in due time the reasons why we formulate the constraint in that way.

We will now discuss Obenauer's claims about *que* in exclamative sentences. Obenauer argues that *que* in sentences like (38)a and (38)b is not a quantifier; his only argument, besides the fact that denying this *que* the status of a quantifier allows him to formulate constraint (40), comes from comparing the distribution of *que* with that of other quantifiers: quantifiers can function as objects, but *que* cannot:

(42) a. Il lui apporte TANT!
       He brings (gives) him so much!

   b. COMBIEN il leur a fait découvrir!
      How much he had them discover!

   c. Elle laissera TOUT à son amant.
      She will leave everything to her lover.

(43) *Qu'il leur a apporté!
     How much he gave them!

Consequently *que* is not a quantifier! This sort of gap in the paradigm of *que* shouldn't however be used to argue against the quantifier nature of *que* in exclamatives. It only shows that when the quantifier *que* is part of a NP, the head of the NP must be lexically realized. Something similar exists for *quel*, the only difference being that *quel* may not be separated from the head noun.

(44) a. Quel garcon as-tu rencontré?
       Which boy did you meet?

   b. *Quel as-tu rencontré?
      *Which did you meet?

The fact that *quel* may not appear without a head is not a reason for saying that in (44)b it is not a determiner. Notice that examples like (44)b were grammatical in the XVIth century.

(45) Je n'y voy qu'un inconvenient. - ... Et QUEL?
     I see only one drawback to it. - ... And which one?
     (Rabelais, II, 15, in Huguet, Vol. 6:274)

The relevance of this is that at the same time that (45) was good, (46)a was good too, i.e. *quel* could be the head of a partitive construction, while this is no longer possible, as shown in (46)b:

(46) a. Par quel des deux sens vérifierons-nous sa véritable essence que nous cherchons? (Montaigne, II, 12 (II, 373) in Huguet, VI:275)
       By which one of the two senses will we verify its true essence which we are looking for?

   b. *Quel de tes amis est venu?
      Which one of your friends came?

This suggests that a DETERMINER of an NP may appear alone on the surface (and by ALONE I mean without a head noun next to it or somewhere else in the sentence) if it may appear as the head of a partitive construction: *tant, combien, lequel* can be the head of a partitive construction and can occur alone also, and *quel* and *que* cannot. (This doesn't account for *tout* and *tous* which can occur alone, but not as the head of a partitive construction; they have to be considered separately anyway, being prearticles). Very tentatively one could account for (43) and (44)b by excluding deep structures like (47), where Det will have to be adequately defined:

(47)   *[Det [Δ]]
        X^n X^{n-1}

This will have to be made more precise, but it seems on the right track to me. Notice that it would account for the distribution of the *quelques* (some) and *chaque* (each) also:

(48) a. QUELQUES ÉTUDIANTS sont en retard.

Some students are late.

b. *QUELQUES sont en retard

Some are late.

c. *QUELQUES DES ÉTUDIANTS sont en retard.

Some of the students are late.

(49) a. CHAQUE ÉTUDIANT est en retard.

Each student is late.

b. *CHAQUE est en retard.

Each is late.

c. *CHAQUE DES ÉTUDIANTS est en retard.

Each of the students is late.

In addition, there is one sort of exclamative sentence where it is clear that the *que* is a quantifier. Consider the following examples, from Obenauer (1976:126, 130):

(50) a. Que de chevelus sont arrivés!

How many long haired people came!

b. Que de poils vous avez sur la poitrine!

How much hair you have on your chest!

The null hypothesis would be to consider *que* as a quantifier here, by analogy with *beaucoup*, *peu*, *tellement*, etc., in examples like *beaucoup de chevelus*, *tellement de poils*. Obenauer claims on the contrary that the *que* in (50)a and (50)b is the complementizer and that the quantifier in exclamatives introduced by *que* has no phonological realization. So the underlying structure of (50)b, for example, would be (51) after application of wh-movement:

(51) [[wh de poils] que] vous avez sur la poitrine
      Comp NP

To obtain (50)b, Obenauer (1976:131) proposes rule (52), which substitutes the complementizer *que* for the null quantifier, the feature wh remaining.

(52) Comp attraction (obligatory):

[wh X que] → [$\genfrac{}{}{0pt}{}{que}{wh}$ X ∅]
Comp

Such a rule is extremely suspicious: it inserts an item of a certain category (complementizer) into the position of another category, QP (in the case of exclamatives) or NP (in the case of questions). The result of the output of this rule is thus that *que* in exclamatives is dominated by QP and in questions by NP! This seems to be what the analysis was fighting against. Evidently, one could agree with Obenauer that *que* in (38) is a complementizer, and not subscribe to all the details of his analysis, for example one may reject rule (52). I see no way that Obenauer's analysis can be defended for (50)a-b, and there is in fact independent evidence that *que* is a quantifier there. Gérard (1977) has shown in her very detailed study of exclamation in French that there are cases where *que* could not be a complementizer, since there was no sentence in the examples involved, and *que* could only be considered as a quantifier. She gives the following examples (Gérard, 1977:187, 191, 32):

(53) a. Que d'eau!

       What a big amount of water!

   b. Que d'histoires pour pas grand chose!

       Such a lot of stories for nothing!

   c. Elle ne vous suffit pas, non, la caution morale --
       et que significative! --du sweater tricoté par Mme
       Delorme mère?[3] (Berthelon, 1955:24)

       It is not enough for you, no, the moral guarantee --
       and how significant! -- of the sweater knitted by
       Ms. Delorme?

Gérard argues that it is unlikely that the exclamations in such examples should be derived from reduced sentences, which would leave some hope to someone who would like to maintain that even here *que* is not a complementizer.[4]

We can now come back to one aspect of the constraint given in (41). Notice that the structural description of the constraint is not as in (54).

(54)   [... [[que]...]...]
       S   S̄ Comp

with *que* exhaustively dominated by Comp. Some facts suggest that the structural description given in (54) is too restrictive, at least for some speakers.

Consider the following example, mentioned by Gérard (1977:156):

(55)   Regarde, mon enfant, que de sottises tu as dites en cinq minutes!

   See, my child, how many stupid things you said in five minutes!
                         (Sandfeld, 1936:58)

Such examples certainly exist, and they are excluded by (41). There is however a clear difference for all speakers between examples such as (55), with the embedded clause separated from the embedding verb by a parenthetical, and examples such as (56), that Gérard considers as grammatical; all my informants reject these examples with exclamative interpretation:

(56)   a.   Tu imagines que de trésors on a perdus!

            You imagine how many treasures we lost!

       b.   Vois que peu d'espoir il nous reste!

            See how little hope is left for us!

       c.   Ils ne savent pas que triste est la vie![5]

            They don't know how sad life is!

For speakers who accept such examples, under the relevant reading, (54) may have to replace the structural description given in (41). For those people who reject (56) with the exclamative readings, Obenauer's constraint is not general enough and (41) gives the right result.

To conclude this section: Obenauer tried to show that facts such as in (35)b, (37)b, and (38)b couldn't be accounted for under the hypothesis that considered the *que*'s there as something else than the complementizer *que*. In fact his own account is compatible with the hypothesis that these *que*'s are not complementizers. Moreover, we have seen that his arguments for saying that *que* in exclamatives was not a quantifier were very weak. It is most likely that the *que* in (50) and (53) is a quantifier. In cases like (38)a however more work is necessary before we can reach a well-motivated conclusion about the category to which the *que* belongs.

6.2.4.2 Restrictiveness.

Obenauer's analysis accounts straightforwardly for the fact that it is precisely *que* that we find in questions such as (14)b and (15)b, and it is an automatic consequence of the fact that we find the complementizer *que* only in Comp, and alone. The specific formulation of the *quoi* → *que* rule also accounts for the facts, but it is easy to imagine formulations of the rule that would predict another distribution for *que* if it was an interrogative pronoun (Obenauer, 1976:84-85). This makes Obenauer's analysis preferable at first sight. However, it is not exceptional to find rules which look rather idiosyncratic, especially when the morphological component is involved. French offers a nice example in relative clauses. Consider the following facts:

(57) a. Pierre, DONT LE PÈRE s'appelle André, vient de partir.

   Peter, whose father's name is André, just left.

   b. *Pierre, LE PÈRE DONT s'appelle André, vient de partir.

   Peter, whose father's name is André, just left.

(58) a. Le garçon avec le père de qui je m'entends bien vient de partir.

   b. *Le garçon avec le père dont je m'entends bien vient de partir.

   The boy with whose father I get along well just left.

Kayne (1975a: 44) accounted for the distribution of *dont* by rule (59):

(59)   [[de Pro] -WH] → dont 2

   Comp PP   1   2

This rule ensures that *dont* occurs only in Comp, and alone. The
sort of rule that people have usually assumed to account for the
alternation between *quoi* and *que* in French is thus not the only one
of its kind in the language. More interesting perhaps, is the following. In the XVI and XVIIth centuries *que* was still found in embedded
questions:

(60) J'ignorois que ce pouvait être qui lui coloroit ce
beau teint.

I didn't know what it was that gave him this nice color.
(Malherbe, I, 126, 5 from Haase, 1969:87)

Obenauer assumes that here *que* is a morphological variant of
quoi. But to my knowledge, *que* is never found in another position
than in Comp at the time, i.e. it is not found in post-verbal position in multiple or echo-question. If it is correct that *que* was a
wh-word at the time, a rule of the sort of (26) was thus already
necessary.

6.2.4.3 *Que and case*.

The traditional view considers *que* as a morphological variant
of *quoi* coming from a direct object position; given the existence
of cases where *que* corresponds to a subject gap in an embedded
sentence, as in (61)a (Obenauer, 1976:109) and (61)b (Hirschbühler,
1976:258), it seems that *que* shouldn't be characterized as the object
form of *quoi* (but see Goldsmith, 1978:12-13 , for how one could still
mark *que* here as [-nominative]):[6]

(61) a. QUE crois-tu qui est tombé?

What do you think fell?

b. QUE crains-tu qui se passe?

What do you fear happened?

Obenauer says that his analysis doesn't have to deal with the problem
of an 'object' form corresponding to a subject. But in fact, as
statement (26) shows, the morphological variant view doesn't have
to make reference to 'object' either.[7]

6.2.4.4 The *que/qui* alternation in questions.

Obenauer's analysis automatically accounts for why (62)a is
ungrammatical, since, if *que* is the complementizer, the *que* → *qui*
rule will apply and generate (62)a, which is also ungrammatical under
the intended reading:

(62) a. *Qu'est tombé?

b. *Qui est tombé?
What fell?

Obenauer (1976:110-111) proposes, following a suggestion from Kayne, that there might be an interpretive rule specifying that the complementizer *qui* introducing questions can only be interpreted as [+human] He then says that under the traditional view one needs some ad hoc condition to exclude subjects which have the form *que* (in fact only *que*'s adjacent to the trace they leave), or exclude *quoi* if it is not changed into a *que*, as in (63):

(63) *Quoi se passe?
What is happening?

If we assume that there is no *qui* in the paradigm of the inanimates, the traditional analysis will not generate (62)b.[8] A constraint like (64) will then be enough to exclude (62)a:

(64) *[que [[e]...]]

    NP

This completes our review of Obenauer's arguments as far as tensed sentences are concerned. I refer the reader to Goldsmith (1978) for additional criticisms.

In the next part we will try to make some aspects of the traditional analysis more precise and adequate than the simple version given earlier. Some of the suggestions that will be made come from ongoing research done by Goldsmith: he shouldn't be held responsible for the use I made of his present suggestions, which may take a rather different form as his work progresses.

6.2.5 *Que* as a pronoun.

I have suggested that the distribution of *que* in tensed interrogative clauses could be accounted for by a rule like (26), repeated here:

(26) [quoi] → [que]

    Comp   Comp

As pointed out by Goldsmith (1978:11-12), if *que* is an allomorph of the morpheme QUOI the choice between *quoi* and *que* will be done in the morphological component, based on what the surface structure as produced by the syntax is. This is also how the choice between *moi* and *me* is done:

(65) a. Pierre ME regarde.   Peter is looking at me.

b. Pierre ne regarde que MOI.   Peter is looking only at me.

It is a well-known fact that *que* in direct questions (as well as *quel*, in direct and indirect questions) behaves as a clitic, since it cannot be separated from the verb by anything else than the negation and the object clitics: it may not be separated from the verb by an adverb, a NP, a parenthetical clause, or even by the subject clitic, as the following examples, from Obenauer, show:

(66) a. *Que, a ton avis, va-t-il se passer maintenant?

What, according to you, is going to happen now?

b. *Que Marie cherche-t-elle?

What is Mary looking for?

c. *Que tu cherches?[9]

What are you looking for?

How can we distinguish the clitic pronouns from the non-clitic ones? In her thesis, Selkirk (1972:217) proposes that "pronominal clitics do not have their own word boundaries", just as "articles do not have word boundaries of their own" (Selkirk, 1972:209). On page 154 she also introduces rule (67):

$$(67) \quad \left[\# \begin{bmatrix} + \text{PRO} \\ + \text{personal} \\ - \text{emphatic} \\ - \text{possessive} \end{bmatrix}_{N''} \# \right]_{N''} \rightarrow \left[\begin{bmatrix} + \text{PRO} \\ + \text{personal} \\ - \text{emphatic} \\ - \text{possessive} \end{bmatrix}_{N''} \right]_{N''}$$

And she adds convention (68) (p. 154):

(68) Define as a syntactic dependent any item not bounded by word boundaries.

Let us add that a syntactic dependent must be in a certain position with respect to some head; the details of this, though relevant, won't be discussed here. For some proposals, see Selkirk (1972: 43-52).

Selkirk (1972:42, 154-155) also adds:

(69) All non-lexical categories are syntactic dependents.

It is then possible to account for (65)a if we start with a postverbal *moi* and let the convention (67) apply, so that the word boundaries are erased, and then define cliticization on items not bounded by word boundaries.[10]

The morphological component specifies what allomorph of a certain morpheme is chosen in what environment. This sort of approach can be made in the case of the *quoi/que* alternation if we adopt Goldsmith's suggestion that there exists a language particular rule in French deleting word boundaries around *quoi* in a specific environment. I include *diable* in the rule. *Diable* may be considered as a suffix which attaches to wh-words: a better understanding of the semantics of *-diable* may explain why it occurs only with a wh-phrase in COMP in questions. One alternative would be not to include it here, if it is possible, as suggested by Obenauer (1976:120), to insert *diable* in its surface position relatively late, i.e., in his description, after PAS-DE-QUOI, and in ours, after the rule which deletes word boundaries around QUOI.

(70) [# QUOI (diable) #] → Ø 2 3 Ø
 Comp
       1   2   3   4

We may then assume that the morphological component contains the information that the allomorph of QUOI without word boundaries around it is *que*. As far as cliticization is concerned two lines are possible: one would be to have a rule Chomsky-adjoining *que* to the verb, just as Kayne (1975b:92 sqq) does for the subject clitic. In fact it is possible to suggest that *que* is moved into the subject clitic slot, accounting in this way for why examples such as (66)c are ungrammatical. Another possibility would be along the lines proposed by Selkirk in her dissertation to account for the subject clitic: it occupies the subject position, but the absence of boundaries around it is enough to account for liaison phenomena (p. 208) and I assume that the impossibility of inserting material between this subject clitic and the verb and its satellites would follow from the structural relation that may exist between a syntactic dependent and the head of a construction (see Selkirk, 1972: 42-54): the presence of material between the clitic subject and the verb would prevent the adequate relation from existing and the result would be excluded by some convention. The same approach could thus be taken for *que*. We will make this more precise with one example:

(71) Que mange Pierre?
      What is Peter eating?

Let us assume the following deep structure:

(72) [#[que] [# [# [# [# Pierre #] #] #]
      S̄ Comp   S NP N' N   N N' NP

      [# [# [# mange #] [# [# [# QUOI #] #] #] #] #] #] #]
      VP V' V   V NP N' N   N N' NP V' VP S S̄

The distribution of word boundaries in deep structure is done according to a variant of a *SPE* convention, as stated in Selkirk (1972:14):

(73) The boundary # is automatically inserted at the beginning
and end of every string dominated by a major category,
i.e., by one of the lexical categories 'noun', 'verb',
'adjective', or by a category such as 'sentence', 'noun
phrase', 'verb phrase', which dominates a lexical category,
whether the phrase category be present in the base or
introduced by a transformation.

$\bar{S}$ also triggers the # boundary to be introduced.

After the application of (i) wh-movement, (ii) stylistic inversion of the subject, which we assume, does not leave a trace -- or, according to Selkirk, word boundaries -- and (iii) complementizer *que* deletion, we can apply a second convention from *SPE*, as formulated by Selkirk (1972:12):

(74) *SPE* II

In a sequence W#] #] Z   or W[# [#Z, where $Y \neq \bar{S}$,
                           X Y   Y X

delete the inner word boundary.

We get then:

(75) [#[[#[[QUOI]]#]][#[[[manger].......#]
     $\bar{S}$ Comp   S VP V V $\bar{S}$

Rule (70) can then be applied. We depart here from Selkirk (1972: 226) who assumes that language particular # deletions and insertions occur before *SPE* II. We can maintain Selkirk's suggestion if we formulate (70) as deleting all the # boundaries in [...QUOI...]. Once again, the exact details of the analysis will need more work.

At that moment, this QUOI meets one of the conditions for being a syntactic dependent (see (68)). Let us assume that it is at this time that the choice of *que* as the right allomorph is made, so we can get *que (diable)*. Only one word boundary is going to separate *que (diable)* and the following verb, and I assume this will allow *que* and *que diable* to be in the proper environment to totally satisfy the condition for them to be syntactic dependents of the VERB. The fact that (66)c, repeated below, is ungrammatical, may perhaps be used to argue that a phrase in COMP is not in the appropriate place to be a dependent of the verb it c-commands and that in sentences such as (66)d, *que* occupies the position occupied earlier by the subject clitic, as the result of a readjustment rule, whether that position is the NP slot dominated by S or a position under V.

(66) c. *Que tu cherches?

　　　d. Que cherches-tu?

I won't explore these possibilities here.

We may turn now to some apparent problems which can be illuminated by some other principles proposed by Selkirk for data not related to the *quoi/que* alternation.

Obenauer (1976:100-101) points out something which he thinks is a problem for the hypothesis that *que* is a clitic pronoun: when it is modified by *diable*, it can be separated from the verb by a subject NP or by a parenthetical clause; *que diable* is thus not a clitic. This was already pointed out by Moignet (1974b:175 sqq) and Kayne (1972:114). We thus have the following facts:

(76) a. *Que Marie cherche-t-elle?

　　　　What is Mary looking for?

　　 b. Que diable Marie cherche-t-elle?

　　　　What the hell is Mary looking for?

　　 c. Que diable, à ton avis, Marie cherche-t-elle?

　　　　What the hell, according to you, is Mary looking for?

In addition, according to Obenauer, one would then expect sentences like (77) to be grammatical:

(77) a. *Que diable d'intéressant a-t-il proposé?

　　　　What the hell which is interesting did he propose?

　　 b. *Que diable qui mérite d'être retenu a-t-elle dit?

　　　　What the hell which deserves to be remembered did she say?

For Obenauer, the fact that (76)b and (76)c are grammatical while (77)a and (77)b are not shows that two factors play a role in *que* having clitic properties and that its clitic-like character does not have the same status as that of personal pronouns. He concludes that the parallelism that the pronominalist hypothesis claims there is between *que/quoi* and the clitic/non-clitic personal pronouns is doubtful.[11]

My first comment is that I am able to find only one factor
that determines whether *que* is going to be a clitic or not: it
is a clitic if it is not modified at all, otherwise not. The second
point is that examples like (77) will never be generated at all since
the rule deleting word boundaries around *QUOI* (*diable*) in Comp,
and which determines the choice of the allomorph *que* when it is
applied, doesn't apply when there is any other material than *QUOI*
(*diable*) in Comp. The only thing that remains to be explained is
why there is no cliticization in (76)b and (76)c, and why the result
is grammatical. The behavior of *que diable* can be explained by
Selkirk's Polysyllabic Non-Lexical Category Rule (1972:217):

(78) <u>Polysyllabic Non-Lexical Category Rule</u> (Poly NLC)

$$[C_0 V C_0 V C_0 X] \rightarrow [\#C_0 V C_0 V C_0 X\#]$$

This rule adds word boundaries around polysyllabic non-lexical items.
This rule accounts for the difference in behavior with respect to
liaison between polysyllabic and monosyllabic non-lexical items in
French (Selkirk, 1972:Chapter III). Selkirk also points out that a
distinction must be made in Russian and in Italian between polysyllabic and monosyllabic non-lexical items; for example, in Italian,
only monosyllabic pronouns can cliticize to the beginning of the verb.

Let us thus assume that Selkirk's Poly NLC applies after rule (70),
which we choose here to apply after *SPE* II, and after the choice of
the appropriate allomorph has been made. And let us assume in addition
that at that time *que(diable)* is still in Comp. We may then represent
the relevant part of (76)b by (79):

(79) [#[[# [[que]diable]#]][#[[[Marie]]#]
    S̄ Comp NP N'   N   S NP N'   N

    [# [[cherche].....]
    VP V' V   S̄

Here, *que diable* is bounded by word boundaries and can thus no
longer be a syntactic dependent. It can't cliticize as a result
and the subject NP, or a parenthetical clause, or an adverb, can
separate it from the verb. *Que diable* may however not be separated
from the verb by the subject pronoun in direct questions, contrary
to what we might first expect:

(80) a. *Que diable tu veux que je fasse?
        What the hell do you want me to do?

(80) b. *Que diable tu as acheté?
What the hell did you buy?

Notice first that it is not the case that the subject clitic pronoun must obligatorily be inverted in direct questions, at least in colloquial speech (see fn. 9):

(81) a. Qui tu veux que j'invite?
Who do you want me to invite?

b. Comment tu as fait?
How did you do?

As Goldsmith pointed out to me, the ungrammaticality of (80) has nothing to do with *que diable* in particular: in direct questions, when *diable* follows a wh-word, subject clitic inversion or stylistic inversion must apply (facts are different, I think, in exclamative clauses):

(82) a. Qui tu as invité?
Who did you invite?

b. Qui diable as-tu invité?

c. *Qui diable tu as invité?
Who the hell did you invite?

(83) a. Où Paul s'en va?
Where is Paul going?

b. Où diable Paul s'en va-t-il?

c. Où diable s'en va Paul?

d. *Où diable Paul s'en va?
Where the hell is Paul going?

We thus don't have to restrict Poly NLC in any way to account for (79).

Let us recapitulate what we have seen. The analysis we have given covers the facts seen until now, and actually, it covers more facts than Obenauer's analysis, since we account for cliticization of *que* along the lines first suggested by Goldsmith as well as for the non-cliticization of *que diable*. To do this we have made use

of a variety of conventions and rules, some of which are well-known
(the *SPE* conventions), some of which Selkirk postulated to account
for several facts from French and other languages; see (67), (68),
(69), (73), (74), (78). We have also proposed the language-parti-
cular rule (70) and we have made some assumptions about ordering
between the choice of the correct allomorph of QUOI and rule (79).
Variations on this analysis are undoubtedly possible, and more work
is necessary to try to justify independently some of the decisions
we have made (or to replace them with better ones).

We can now add one reason to our decision to formulate rule
(41), without mentioning Comp: it is not clear that interrogative
que is in Comp; it may be attached to the verb: this is at least
a possibility in the case of direct questions where it is clear that
que behaves like a clitic. We have made the assumption that
interrogative *que* has the same behavior in embedded clauses as in
main clauses; if for some reason our hypothesis proves to be incorrect and interrogative *que* should not cliticize in indirect questions,
then COMP could be introduced, in the formulation of (41), i.e. the
relevant structure would be as in (54); for those who consider the
examples in (56) as ungrammatical, the relevant structure would be
as in (84):

(84) [... [[que X]] ......]
       S   COMP

The S label on the outer brackets ensures that the COMP in (84)
belongs to an embedded clause.

6.3 Infinitival clauses

6.3.1 Introduction

Discussion of infinitival questions seems more difficult in
some respects to me because of the intuition that they sound somewhat
archaic. This holds especially for direct questions. Keeping this
in mind, let us consider the facts as they are described by Obenauer
first.

6.3.2 *QUE* and *QUOI* in Main Clauses

According to Obenauer (1976:113 sqq, 1977:319) *que* is preferred
to *quoi* in direct infinitival questions; he reports the following
judgments:

(85) a. ??Quoi lui offrir pour sa fête?

b. Que lui offrir pour sa fête?
What to offer him for his birthday?

(86) a. ??Quoi répondre à cette question?

b. Que répondre à cette question?
What to answer to this question?

(87) a. ??Quoi construire sur ce terrain?

b. Que construire sur ce terrain?
What to build on this piece of land?

I agree with Obenauer that *que* is preferred to *quoi*, at least at first sight. I don't find the a examples quite as bad as his informants apparently do. The difference between the a and b examples seems somewhat a difference in style, *que* being more literary; the first reaction is also that the b examples aren't requests for information.

6.3.3 QUE and QUOI in embedded sentences

Obenauer (1976:113, 1977:318) reports the opposite sort of judgments with respect to the quality of *que* and *quoi* in embedded clauses.

(88) a. Je me demande quoi lui offrir pour sa fête.

b. *?Je me demande que lui offrir pour sa fête.
I am wondering what to offer him for his birthday.

(89) a. Je ne sais pas quoi répondre à cette question.

b. *Je ne sais pas que répondre à cette question.
I don't know what to answer to this question.

(90) a. J'ignore quoi construire sur ce terrain.

b. *J'ignore que construire sur ce terrain.
I don't know what to build on this piece of land.

Here my judgments are identical to those offerred.

Obenauer adds that *que* with *je ne sais* ('I don't know', with the second member of the negation, i.e. *pas*, missing) is often good, but the quality depends on the complement of *savoir*.

So, while (91)a-b are perfect, the examples in (92) are not (for additional examples, see Obenauer, 1976:113, fn. 43, and 1977: 318, fn. 23):

(91) a. Je ne sais que faire.

   I don't know what to do.

   b. Je ne sais qu'en dire.

   I don't know what to say about it.

(92) a. ?Je ne sais QUE prêter à Pierre.

   I don't know what to lend to Peter.

   b. ?Je ne sais QUE nationaliser dans ce pays.

   I don't know what to nationalize in this country.

   c. ?Je ne sais QUE repasser.

   I don't know what to iron.

   d. ?Je ne sais QU' infliger à mes ennemis.

   I don't know what to inflict on my enemies.

Quoi is perfect in (92), while doubtful in (91), according to Obenauer; I find it perfect in this last case.[12]

Assuming for the sake of the discussion that *quoi* is found in embedded clauses only, and *que* in main clauses only, let us look at Obenauer's analysis.

6.3.4 Obenauer's analysis

As might be expected, Obenauer claims that *quoi* in the embedded clauses is the question word, while *que* in the main clauses is the complementizer.

Let us consider embedded clauses first.

Remember the formulation of PAS-DE-QUOI:

(93) [QUOI X que] → ∅ 2

   Comp   1   2

As the rule indicates, *QUOI X* can be deleted only if the complementizer *que* is present in COMP. Kayne (1974:315a) has argued that the complementizer *que* was associated only with sentences whose main verb was in a finite tense.[13] Obenauer takes advantage of this: since there is no *que* in infinitival clauses, at least at the moment of application of PAS-DE-QUOI, this rule won't erase *QUOI*, explaining why we get the a version of (88)-(90), and not the b version. In those cases like (90) where *que* is accepted, it is considered as an historical remnant, mainly literary, of an earlier usage, where *que* was still a pronoun (1976:116, 1977:318, fn. 23).[14]

Let us turn to direct infinitival questions. Obenauer suggests that in fact *que* is excluded only from embedded infinitival clauses (1976:116). One way he suggests to do this is to have the complementizer *que* with both tensed and non-tensed clauses at some moment, and to delete *que* in the case of embedded infinitival clauses by a transformation distinct from QUE-deletion (see 7d); this transformation, QUE-NON, which would have to refer to [+infinitival] in some way, must precede PAS-DE-QUOI (Obenauer, 1976:122). There isn't however the slightest independent evidence that *que* is present as a complementizer at any stage of the derivation of direct infinitival questions, and unless some additional mechanism is provided, the assumption that the complementizer *que* is present in infinitival direct questions makes a wrong prediction for non-standard French. It is well-known that in some varieties of non-standard French, both the wh-word and the complementizer *que* can be found together. The distribution in headed relatives is a little different from that in free relatives and questions. Only that in questions is relevant here: we may find NP, PP, AdvP in front of *que*:

(94)   A qui qu'elle a parlé?

   To whom did she speak?

   Qui que tu as vu?

   Who did you see?

   Comment qu'il s'appelle?

   What is his name?

If, as Obenauer claims (1977:324) the difference here between standard and non-standard French is that both PAS-DE-QUOI and QUE-deletion are obligatory in the first case and not in the second one, we would expect to find examples such as the following ones in non-standard French:

(95) a. *A qui que parler?
   *Who to speak to?

   b. *Qui que voir?
   *Who to see?

   c. *Comment que faire?
   *How to do?

Such examples are totally out (the English translations are ungrammatical but remember that the French examples without *que* are grammatical), and similar examples have never been found at any period of French where we have examples of wh-words and complementizer *que* cooccurring in Comp. So, while Obenauer (1977:320) considers that infinitival questions give support to his contention that *que* in questions is the complementizer, because the allomorphic approach would, according to him, need some ad hoc condition blocking the choice of *que* in infinitival embedded questions in favor of *quoi*, I think that the fact that *que* is found in direct infinitival questions should really be considered as a major problem for his analysis.

In the next section we will examine Gougenheim's observations (1970) on the distribution of *que* and *quoi* in infinitival questions.

6.3.5 Gougenheim's insights [15]

The first observation made by Gougenheim (1970c:124) is that the use of *quoi* with an infinitive comes from Old French, where a verb in the infinitive could not be preceded by an unstressed, a weak, pronoun. As French changed, the weak form of the personal pronouns generalized in front of infinitives, but interrogative *quoi* kept being possible, concurrently with *que*. This is not very important for an analysis of present day French, except in that it may convince us that making use of the distinction between finite and non-finite tense in order to account for the distribution of *quoi* and *que* is not necessarily ad hoc. Obviously the extent to which this distinction may play a role in present-day French, as compared to the usefulness of this distinction in Old French, may not be very important, but languages have rules of limited generality too, especially as the result of historical changes.

The second sort of observation made by Gougenheim is much more interesting, though it is difficult to make it extremely precise. Looking at the distribution of *quoi* and *que* (as direct objects) he argues that there is a semantic difference correlated with the choice of *que* rather than *quoi* in infinitival clauses. In a very imprecise way, it could be said that *que* tends to be used to express embarrassment, while *quoi* tends to be used when there is a real request for information, or when the information matters. We will try to make this a little less vague by looking at Gougenheim's examples.

The first sort of example comes from dialogues:

(96) a. Je m'en vais en Norvège -Quoi faire?

I am going to Norway- To do what?

Here, it is clear that *que* cannot be used. The reason, according to Gougenheim, is that the questioner really wanted to know what the other person was going to do in Norway, i.e. it had to do with a concrete occupation, and not with having to take some decision (p. 136) So, if we had had the dialogue (97), the person who would have asked the question would just have expressed the fact that he didn't know what to do, given this news.

(97) Je m'en vais en Norvège. -Que faire?

I am going to Norway - What shall I do?

Moignet (1974:174) gave the name DELIBERATIVE questions to infinitival questions (he didn't distinguish the case of *quoi* and *que*). This name seems particularly appropriate in the case of *que* .

It could however be suggested that the difference between (96) and (97) is that the question in (96) is really an embedded question, i.e. the question is sort of a reduced sentence.

Let us take another example discussed by Gougenheim (1970c:125-6):

(98) Ah! ces passions! quoi leur opposer? que faire pour lutter contre leur torrent furieux? (Maurice Donnay, Dialogues d'hier, 49).

According to him, *quoi leur opposer?* means *quelle digue, quelle barrière peut-on opposer aux passions*? ("what dikes, what barrier can one oppose to passions?") while *que faire*? is more general and vague: *de quelle façon peut-on agir*? ("how can one act?"). The difference here is subtle, and I wouldn't be surprised if some people would disagree, especially since in both cases it is implied that there is nothing that one can do against passions. The difference I make is this: it seems that with 'quoi leur opposer?', none of the concrete means that one could think of would be of any use, while in the next question it seems that no concrete means of action is considered at all. Very often, the difference is difficult to see, especially outside of context. This difference between *quoi* and *que* may explain the difference in judgment between (91)a-b

and (92): the more general the VP following *je ne sais* is, the
better the result. This is in no way precise, unfortunately. It
explains also why some of the examples at least are not (much) better
as direct questions than as indirect ones. One reason also why it
is difficult to use *quoi-* in direct questions is that the TYPICAL
use of infinitival direct questions is not to ask information, but
is to express embarrassment. It is in fact its only use in English,
where this sort of question is very marginal.

If Gougenheim is right when he considers that *Quoi faire?* in
general means something like *A quelle occupation me livrerai-je?*
(or *te livreras-tu?, se livrera-t-elle?*) while *que faire?* only
expresses the embarrassment in which somebody is to make any kind
of decision, then it is expected that adding something to the question
which indicates that some concrete action is going to be taken will
preclude the use of *que*, Barbara Hall Partee pointed out to me. This
prediction is correct: (99)a is much better than (99)b, even though
we have a direct question, where, according to Obenauer, *que* is the
regular form and *quoi* is marginal:

(99) a. QUOI faire en premier (tout d'abord)?

   b. ??Que faire en premier (tout d'abord)?

   What shall we do first?

In the case of embedded questions, why is *que* better with 'je ne
sais' than with 'je ne sais pas', 'je sais', or other verbs? Gougenheim
(1970c:126) says that *ne pas savoir* implies more clearly ignorance
than *ne savoir*, and for example ignorance concerning concrete knowledge.
So 'Je ne sais l'anglais' (I don't know English), 'je ne sais pas
nager' (I can't swim). Then, according to Gougenheim, one can conceive
that 'ne pas savoir', relating to a concrete realization, be associated
to *quoi*, while 'ne savoir' would tend to be associated to *que*. This
should be made more precise, and I am unable to come up with something
better at the moment, but I think that Gougenheim was on the right
track. Let us give a last and very clear example of this. He
says (p. 127) that a man who finds himself in a difficult situation
will express his embarrassment by saying 'Je ne sais que faire',
while a child who gets bored will say: 'Je ne sais pas quoi faire'.
For me, the statement about the child is correct; I think it is
possible to use the second example in the first situation; there may
be little differences then in implications. It is quite plausible
that for me, and probably for others, *quoi*, in some environments,
can have the two uses that we have discussed, while *que* may be
restricted to the embarrassment situation, the deliberative use.

I refer the reader to Gougenheim (1970c) for additional examples and discussions. I believe his contribution is essential for understanding the use of *quoi* and *que* in infinitival questions. In the next section we will see how we can incorporate his contribution in our rules.

6.3.6 The rules for *que* and *quoi*

We will give two sorts of analyses, one more in line with the approach that was prevalent before *Filters and Control* (Chomsky and Lasnik, 1977), the other more in line with this work.

6.3.6.1 Analysis 1

In the first analysis I suggest distinguishing clauses in a finite tense from those in a non-finite tense.

(100)   QUE-1 (obligatory)

[# QUOI (diable) #] (NP) V →   Ø 2 3 Ø 5 6
Comp   [+Finite]
 1   2   3   4   5 6

As the result of the application of (100), *que* is chosen. I also assume that the presence of *diable* results in the application of rule (78), which reinserts a pair of word boundaries around polysyllabic non-lexical items; *que diable* does no longer qualify as a syntactic dependent and does not have to cliticize. I will assume that when cliticized, *que* becomes morphologically part of the verb. If anything prevents *que* from becoming part of the verb, the result is excluded by convention: a syntactic dependent which cannot become part of what it is a dependent of makes a sentence ungrammatical. In fact we only need a filter like (101):

(101)   *[que   ]

        Comp   +Q

I assume +Q to be a feature distinguishing questions from exclamatives and relatives. This may have to be modified later, when free relatives are taken into account. We may need something like [+wh, -quantifier]. For the infinitives we would need a rule like (102):

(102)   QUE- 2 (Optional)

[# QUOI (diable) #] V →   Ø 2 3 Ø 5
Comp   [-Finite]
 1   2   3   4   5

If the rule is applied, *que* is chosen, and it must be cliticized on the verb i.e., there is some restructuring rule which must operate.

Depending on whether *quoi* or *que* is chosen, two different rules of interpretation may be used. More probably, the same rule interprets the question, for example along the lines indicated in the first chapter, but different implications would be associated with the question starting with *que* and that starting with *quoi*.

6.3.6.2 Analysis 2

The second analysis will have a very simple statement for the boundary deletion, plus a filter.

(103) QUOI/QUE rule (Optional)

[# QUOI (diable) #] → Ø 2 3 Ø
Comp
 1   2   3   4

The allomorph chosen when (103) applies is *que*. When the rule is not applied, the allomorph chosen is *quoi*. In the first case if *que* can't cliticize, the result is excluded by (101); if *quoi* is chosen, the result is excluded by (104):

(104) QUOI-filter

*[quoi](NP) V

Comp   [+finite]

The rest is the same: we need two rules of interpretation for the *que/quoi* alternation in infinitival questions.

6.3.6.3 Base generation

More and more we find analyses where everything, or nearly everything, is generated in the position that it occupies in surface structure. It is possible that *que* could be generated immediately with the verb and *que diable* could be generated only in COMP (just like *que diable* would). With base-generated traces and rules of co-indexing along the lines of McCloskey (1978) and Bresnan and Grimshaw (1978), there shouldn't be too much problem to ensure proper interpretation. Filters like (104), (101), and others if necessary, would exclude the ungrammatical sentences. I leave this approach for another occasion.

6.4 Inanimate *qui* in the XVIth-XVIIIth centuries

We have seen in 6.2.4.4, where examples such as (105) were agrammatical, those cases where one forces an inanimate interpretation on *qui*:

(105) *Qui est tombé?

　　　What fell?

A large number of examples of that kind is however found from the XVIth to the XVIIIth century. I haven't looked at earlier periods Gougenheim (1970b) looked in detail at all the examples from the XVIIth and XVIIIth centuries he could find and we will discuss only those. Since we have questions, how do we know that *qui* is intended to refer to inanimates? We know it by the context or by the answer.

(106)　Seigneur, QUI vous ramène? Est-ce l'impatience
　　　　D'ajouter à mes maux ceux de votre présence?

　　　　　　(Corneille, *Pulcherie*, III, 13, in Gougenheim, 1970b:115)

　　　　My lord, WHAT brings you back? Is it the impatience to
　　　　add to my problems those of your presence?

Gougenheim gives 33 examples and I refer the reader to his article for more.

What is this *qui*? Along the lines of Obenauer's analysis, one could argue that this *qui* is a complementizer: the *que* → *qui* rule would apply and give *qui*, and French at that period would not have the mechanism that excludes (105), i.e. the rule of interpretation for [qui ...] wouldn't force the [+human] interpretation (see 6.2.4.4
　　　　　$\overline{S}$　+wh

and footnote 9) or present day French could be thought as having filter (107), lacking before the 19th century:

(107)　*[　　[　qui　]　]

　　　　Comp　Complementizer

　　　　If COMP is not co-indexed with some phrase c-commanding
　　　　it (see Bresnan and Grimshaw, 1978, section 2)

The qualification on the filter ensures, assuming wh-movement from COMP to COMP, that if a wh-word has gone through some COMP and ends up in a higher Comp, the Comp below will be co-indexed with that wh-word and the constraint won't be able to apply to it.

There is however good evidence that this *qui* is not the complementizer, but the wh-word, the interrogative pronoun, i.e. that *qui* could be used as an interrogative pronoun for inanimates to a certain extent. The first sort of evidence is very suggestive. Gougenheim observes that in all the examples *qui* could be used as a subject only if the verb accepts [+human] subjects. In addition, the subject had to be seen as behaving in some way as a person: *qui* wasn't used when the action (the event) described resulted simply in something happening to the relevant object (On ne trouve point *qui* lorsqu'il s'agit d'actions dues à l'inertie des choses: qui s'est cassé? qui a été brisé?" Gougenheim (1970b:117)). Notice that in the two examples just given, the verb accepts animate subjects, but the subject is not seen as performing as an animate. Gougenheim suggests that *qui* should be marked as animate, but that the definition of animate for present purposes should be adjusted (see p. 118).

In addition he gives one example where *qui* comes from direct object position:

(108) Je ne sais QUI je dois admirer davantage,

Ou de ce grand amour ou de ce grand courage.

(Corneille, *Illusion Comique*, V, 3, v. 1549, in Gougenheim, 1970b: 118)

I don't know WHAT I should admire most,

this great love or this great courage.

Here *qui* can't be the complementizer *qui* since the environment for the *que* → *qui* rule to apply is not met. At the same period *qui* was often used with inanimate antecedents in relative clauses also:

(109) Un crime par qui Rome obtint sa liberté.

(Corneille, *Cinna*)

A murder by which Rome got its liberty.

Gougenheim shows that this use of *qui* in relative clauses is possible only if the antecedent is assimilated to animates.

Let us end this by mentioning that all the examples given come from literary works. I don't know whether *qui* is found for inanimates in questions in non-literary works.

6.5 Conclusion

In this chapter I have argued that interrogative *que* was a pronoun rather than the complementizer, as argued by Obenauer. I think that little of the force that Obenauer's analysis had remains.

There certainly are problems with the details of the analysis I have defended, but I am confident that they can be worked out with a more restrictive theory about the relations between the syntactic and the morphological component of grammars.

In the next chapter we will discuss free relatives and the analysis defended here will be relevant.

FOOTNOTES TO CHAPTER VI

1. Kayne (1975:29) mentions that Lerch (1925) and Jensen (1973) have held within a non-transformational framework that *que* was not a relative pronoun. Gross (1968:122) and Moreau (1970, 1971) argue that the second occurrence of *qui* in (2)b is not a pronoun, but a complementizer, but they don't extend this to the *qui* in examples like (1)b. Some transformational linguists still don't accept Kayne's analysis of *que* and *qui* in examples like (1)a and (1)b, for example Huot (1974:35, fn. 2) and Milner (1977:36, fn. 1). Kayne's analysis seems the best to me, especially given comparative evidence.

2. A chart sorting out the different *que*'s may be helpful. The heading of each column says in which construction the *que* is found. One example is given for each *que*, the number of the example corresponding to that of the column. In the chart it is indicated who considers the relevant *que* a wh-word or a complementizer.

		Wh-form	Complementizer
1.	Restrictive relative		Kayne, Obenauer, Hirschbühler
2.	Question	Hirschbühler (allomorph of *quoi*)	Obenauer
3.	Exclamative 1	Hirschbühler	Obenauer
4.	Exclamative 2	Hirschbühler (with reservations)	Obenauer
5.	Free relative	Hirschbühler (allomorph of *quoi*)	Obenauer

(1) Le garçon QUE tu vois
    The boy that you see

(2) a. Que fais-tu?
       What are you doing?

    b. *Je me demande QUE tu fais.
       I wonder what you are doing.

(3) a. Que de gens tu as invités!
       How many people you invited!

(3) b. *C'est ahurissant que de gens tu as invités!
It's amazing how many people you invited!

(4) a. Que tu es belle!
How pretty you are!

b. *C'est ahurissant que tu es belle!
It's amazing how pretty you are!

(5) *J'ai acheté que tu as acheté.
I bought what you bought.

3. I don't find the parenthetical exclamation in (53)c very good; this is due to the fact that for me examples such as (i)a are less good than (i)b; in fact I find (i)a ungrammatical:

(i) a. *Que significative est sa contribution!

b. Que sa contribution est significative!
How significant is his contribution!

Examples involving NP's are perfect:

(ii) Il avait dit, et que de fois d'ailleurs, qu'il ne me souhaitait pas de connaître ce qu'il avait connu.
He had said, and how many times in fact, that he didn't wish me to experience what he had experienced.

4. It is still debatable whether *que* in examples like (i)a and especially (i)b is a quantifier or a complementizer:

(i) a. Qu'il a de la chance!
How lucky he is!

b. Qu'il a une belle maison!
What a nice house he has!

Even if *que* here is a complementizer, it doesn't mean that it simply is the *que* which introduces embedded clauses usually. Notice for example that parallel to (i)b we have examples like (ii):

(ii) COMME il a une belle maison!
What a nice house he has!

If *comme* here is a complementizer, it should be indicated in some way that it is a quantifier, and the same thing should be done with the exclamative *que*. It would NOT be strange to have a quantifier-complementizer phonologically identical to the general complementizer *que*, since the first one is also identical to the quantifier *que* found in (iii):

    (iii) Que de gens tu as invités!

           How many people you invited!

It was suggested to me by Goldsmith that the fact that there is no inversion in exclamative clauses could be taken as evidence that *que* in (i)a and (i)b for example is a complementizer: subject clitic inversion is a root transformation that applies in main clauses when the complementizer is absent. So we have contrasts as in (iv):

    (iv) a. Peut-être est-il parti.

          b. Peut-être qu'il est parti.

             Maybe he is gone.

This is accounted for by Goldsmith (1977:92) by the No-complementizer condition, which prevents root-transformations from applying to a root S headed by a complementizer. Since the *que* in direct questions allows subject clitic inversion to apply, this *que* would not be a complementizer.

    The argument about exclamatives doesn't go through, since there is no inversion in exclamatives in these cases where it is clear that what is in Comp is not the complementizer, as in (iii) above and in (v):

    (v) Combien de fois il s'est trompé!

         How many times he made a mistake!

The absence of subject clitic inversion in (some) exclamative sentences must thus be explained in another way.

    5. Example (56)c shouldn't be read with the embedded clause understood as in (i):

    (i) Triste est la vie.

         Life is sad.

6. Goldsmith (1978:12-13) suggests that case marking be done at the surface structure level and that a pronoun be marked [+nominative] when it precedes the VP. The *que* in (61)a and (61)b will be marked as [-nominative] assuming case marking to occur before subject clitic inversion (or attachment to V (see Kayne 1972)) and before Stylistic inversion. This is a reasonable analysis, especially in the light of facts from English pointed out to me by B. H. Partee. The examples are from Jespersen (*MEG*:II, 10.7.3 - 10.7.6) where many others can be found:

(i) a. I have met with women WHOM I really think would like to be married to a poem. (Keats, in *MEG*:II:198)

b. ...said one WHOM Davies later learned was Seavey, the village postmaster (Dreiser, in *MEG*:II:198).

Jespersen insists that it is incorrect that a subject must always be in the nominative. Other examples and additional discussion can be found in Jespersen's *Philosophy of Grammar*: 349-351.

7. If case marking plays a role, the distinction between [+Oblique] and [-Oblique] would be enough. A distinction of that type is necessary in the case of exclamative sentences, in order to account for the opposition between (i)a and (i)b-c (from Gérard, 1977:29):

(i) a. Que de gens il a rencontrés!
   How many people they met!

b. *A que de gens elle a parlé!
   How many people she spoke to!

c. *Avec que d'audace ils m'ont répondu!
   How much boldness they answered me with!

Notice that Grimshaw (1977:31-37) has argued that direct exclamatives couldn't start with a prepositional phrase in English:

(ii) *On what a problem he is working!

The situation is different in French:

(iii) a. Dans quel guêpier il s'est fourré!
   In what a mess he put himself!

b. A travers combien de souffrances il a dû passer!
   Through how many sufferings he must have gone!

Notice also:

(iv) a. *Il m'a répondu, avec que d'audace, que j'étais un idiot.

b. Il m'a répondu, avec combien d'audace, que j'étais un idiot.

He answered me, with so much boldness, that I was an idiot.

8. Alternatively, one may want to let the *que/qui* alternation rule generate (62)b. The result will be ungrammatical because *qui* will have the feature inanimate, but the dictionary entry of *qui* pronoun has it marked animate. Since there is no such *qui*, the sentence will be rejected; or it will be interpreted as animate, i.e. the inanimate reading will never be produced with *qui*. This is similar to Obenauer's proposal.

9. Clitic inversion is preferred anyway with other interrogative pronouns but it is quite common not to do so in spoken language:

(i) Qui tu cherches? Où tu t'en vas?

Who are you looking for? Where are you going?

10. As it is stated, (67) is certainly too general; so for example it treats NP's which are complements of a preposition in exactly the same way as direct objects; but not all objects of a preposition cliticize:

(i) a. Je LEUR parle à tous

I talk to them all.

b. Je suis sorti avec eux (tous)

I went out with them (all)

See Kayne (1975b:134 sqq) for a discussion. What is important for us is not the exact details of Selkirk's analysis, but the general approach in terms of boundary deletion.

11. Additional data is relevant here. Obenauer (1976:86, fn. 7) gives the following examples:

(i) a. Que Pierre aimerait-il que Marie lui donne?
(from Ronat, 1973:202)

b. Que Sakharov critique-t-il et comment? (from *Le Monde*)

(i) c. Que cela veut-il dire? (from the Radio)

Gougenheim (1970:110) also gives (ii), which he finds 'abnormal':

(ii) Mais que la royauté lui eût-elle rapporté, sinon des soucis et des périls? (Marc Helys, translation from Selma Lagerlof, *Les vieux manoirs*, *Le Temple*, Paris: Perrin, 1936, p. 187)

Obenauer reports that his informants like (i)a better than (i)b and (i)c, though none of the examples was found perfect. I like (i)a and (ii) best: in previous unwritten work on the topic of *que* with Goldsmith, we consistently noticed that the best examples always involved gaps in an embedded clause introduced by *que/qui*, i.e. a [+finite] clause. As with *que diable*, the result is ungrammatical if the subject of the main clause is an uninverted clitic, while the inversion may be omitted with other interrogative pronouns in casual speech:

(iii) a. *Que tu aimerais que Marie lui donne?

   b. *Que tu veux que je fasse?

(iv) a. ?Qui tu aimerais que j'invite?

   b. Qui tu veux que j'invite?

I have no judgment in the case of parentheticals and I find the insertion of adverbs ungrammatical.

I won't try to account for this array of facts here.

12. One thing that Obenauer's informants didn't notice (but maybe the facts were different for them or they were never tested on that) is that several of the examples in (92) aren't very good as direct questions either, especially the equivalent of (92)d,e; and in some context *que* seems out of place, while *quoi* seems more appropriate. For example, imagine that a European government starts ruling Europe and that the minister of economy has to make his choice about what industries, etc., he is going to nationalize. In that case I find (i)a much better than (i)b; (i)b looks like a rhetorical question: nothing is worth nationalizing.

(i) a. Quoi nationaliser en France, quoi nationaliser en Allemagne, quoi nationaliser aux Pays-Bas?

   b. Que nationaliser en France, que nationaliser en Allemagne, que nationaliser aux Pays-Bas?

   What to nationalize in France, what to nationalize in Germany, what to nationalize in the Netherlands?

13. For a discussion of some problematic cases, see Kayne (1975a: section VII).

14. Obenauer accounts in the same way for examples like (i), which he considers involve an infinitival free relative (Obenauer, 1977:322):

(i) J'ai trouvé quoi mettre sur le mur.
 I found what to put on the wall.

This is in fact an infinitival indirect question. Notice first that it certainly can be an indirect question, given examples like (ii):

(ii) a. J'ai trouvé qui mettre où: Pelé au centre-avant et Garrincha à l'aile droite.
 I found who to put where: Pelé at the front and Garrincha on the left wing.

b. J'ai trouvé à quoi passer mon temps.
 I found what to spend my time at.

There are no multiple relatives and (ii)b can very clearly be interpreted as an indirect question.

Trouver can take an infinitival headed relative, as shown by (iii):

(iii) J'ai trouvé quelque chose avec quoi réparer ma voiture.
 I found something with what to repair my car.

But, if we try to construct an infinitival free relative with a pronoun that is clearly never found in questions the result is ungrammatical:

(iv) *J'ai trouvé quiconque mettre au travail.
 *I found whoever to put to work.

I don't think that it is possible to defend the position that (iv) is a free relative but that there is some semantic reason accounting for why *quiconque* would be excluded there. Examples like (v), which involve without doubt a free RELATIVE, may at first seem strange, lending possible support to the hypothesis that (iv) would be a free relative excluded for semantic reasons.

(v) J'ai invité quiconque tu as invité.
 I invited whoever you invited.

But in fact, (v) is good and can even be improved upon if we make obvious the generic reading:

    (vi) Pierre invite toujours quiconque tu invites.

           Peter always invites whoever you invite.

It is impossible to make (iv) better.

    It is also possible to show that (i) is not a free relative if we eliminate the indirect question reading, or try to force a free relative reading:

    (vii) a. J'ai trouvé quoi mettre sur le mur sur mon lit.

             I found what to put on the wall (while) sitting on my bed.

         b. *J'ai trouvé quoi mettre sur le mur dans le tiroir de Jean.

             I found what to put on the wall in Jean's drawer.

The a example can only be interpreted as meaning that I got the idea while I was on my bed. The b example is ungrammatical with the intended reading.

CHAPTER VII

FREE RELATIVES

7.0 Introduction

The main goal of this chapter is to examine in some detail one aspect of free relatives, i.e. the question of what position the wh-phrase occupies in that construction.

Two views have been held: the wh-phrase is part of the embedded clause, i.e. it is the COMP position, or it is part of the main clause, i.e. it occupies the antecedent position. The first position has been held by Kuroda (1968), Andrews (1975), Gee (1973), and Chomsky (1973) for English, Quicoli (1973) and Hirschbühler (1976a,b) for Classical Greek, Allen (1977) for one kind of free relative in Old English, Hirschbühler (1976b) for Old and Middle French, and XVIth century Spanish, and Van Riemsdijk (1978) for Dutch, English, and Spanish. The second view was first put forward by Bresnan (1973) for English, then by Hirschbühler (1976a,b) for French, Allen (1977) for another sort of free relative in Old English, Grimshaw (1977) for English, Woolford (1978) for Tok Pisin, Daalder (1977) for Dutch, and Bresnan and Grimshaw for English. Bresnan and Grimshaw extend their analysis to French, Old English, Tok Pisin, and Finnish. Van Riemsdijk (1978) has however come up with compelling evidence that in free relatives in Dutch the wh-phrase is in COMP. One consequence is that Daalder's argument in favor of the hypothesis that the wh-phrase is in the antecedent position in Dutch has lost all its force. I consider that the same argument, which Bresnan, Grimshaw, and Hirschbühler used for some of the languages they looked at, has lost its force in general, whatever the language considered. Additional facts from standard French and Montreal French fit very naturally with the hypothesis that in these languages the wh-phrase is in COMP. Looking at some facts from Spanish, it will appear that a distinction between two kinds of free relatives might be necessary, i.e. between those where the wh-phrase has some quantifier morphology (*quienquiera* 'whoever') and those where we have bare wh-phrases (*quien* 'who'). In the first case we may have real headed relatives, while in the second we may have real headless relatives. We will then have a quick survey of a few languages where the wh-phrase is clearly in COMP. Some problematic data will finally be discussed.

7.1 Free relatives in French. A summary.

In Hirschbühler (1976a,b) it was proposed that free relatives as in (1) should be analyzed as having the wh-word in the antecedent position in surface structure, and that they should be derived from a deep structure similar to (2), where we assume that the *que* complementizer is present in deep structure:

(1) J'ai rencontré qui tu as rencontré.

I met who you met.

(2)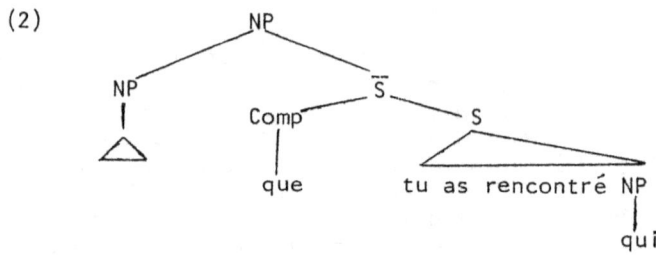

To go from (2) to (1) the following transformations take effect, in the order indicated.

(3) 1. Wh-movement

2. Que-deletion (Chapter VI (7d))

3. Wh-raising

The ordering between the last two operations doesn't have to be stated if these transformations are cyclic. Evidently, the absence of *que* in (1) is accounted for also if *qui* there is really in COMP, since in Standard French a wh-word and the complementizer don't co-occur in COMP in surface structure.

Our claim that the wh-word in such sentences is in the antecedent position in surface structure was prompted by the following type of examples, where the phrase containing immediately the relative clause must be of the same category as the wh-phrase with which it starts. This is what Grimshaw (1977) calls, in a very appropriate manner, the matching effect.

(3) a. [[Qui]ne risque rien]n'a rien.
    NP NP

Who risks nothing gets nothing.

b. [[Qui] j'aime] ne m'aime pas.
    NP NP

Who I love doesn't love me.

c. *[[De qui] j'ai parlé] vient de partir.
    NP PP

About whom I spoke just left.

(4) a. On hait souvent [[qui] n'est pas responsable]
                         NP NP

   One often hates who is not guilty.

   b. Aimez [[qui] j'aime]
             NP NP

   Love who I love

   c. *J'ai rencontré [[à qui] tu m'as dit de parler]
                      NP PP

   I met to whom you told me to speak.

(5) a. Je le dis [[pour qui] je dois le dire]
                   PP PP

   I say it for whom I must say it (for).

   b. J'ai donné ce livre [[à qui] tu avais fait allusion].
                        PP PP

   I gave this book to whom you alluded to.

   c. *Je suis sorti [avec [[à qui] tu as parlé hier]]
                   PP   NP PP

   I went out with to whom you talked yesterday.

(6) a. J'habite [[où] il habite]]
                 Loc Loc

   I live where he lives.

   b. *J'ai acheté [[où] il habite]]
                NP Loc

   I bought where he lives.

As one can see, when the brackets around the wh-phrase and the next pair of brackets have the same label, the sentence is grammatical, otherwise it is not. Some more comments are necessary for examples (5) and (6).

In (5)a-b, one preposition is missing, as can be seen from the parallel examples with the antecedent present:

(7) a. Je le dis POUR celui POUR qui je dois le dire.

    I say it for the one for whom I must say it.

  b. J'ai donné ce livre À celui À qui tu avais fait allusion.

    I gave this book to the one to whom you alluded.

In Hirschbühler (1976a,b) we accounted for such examples by assuming the existence of a preposition deletion rule, which can be formulated as in (8):

(8) $W_1 \; P_i \; P_i \; W_2 \; \rightarrow \; 1 \; 2 \; \emptyset \; 4$
    $\;\;\;\; 1 \;\; 2 \;\; 3 \;\; 4$

One problem with this formulation is that (8) must apply before wh-raising otherwise the wh-NP would separate the two prepositions; i.e. we must first go to the PP level and then go back to the NP which is contained in that PP, assuming a formulation of wh-raising as in (9):

(9) $\Delta_{x^i} \; [\; wh \; W_1 \;] \; W_2 \; \rightarrow \; 2 \; \emptyset \; 3$
    $\;\;\;\;\;\;\;\; 1 \;\;\;\;\;\;\;\; 2 \;\; 3$

Variants of (8) and (9) are possible which avoid that problem (Hirschbühler, 1976a:145). A rule such as (8) looked plausible to us given the existence of a similar rule in Ancient Greek: if the wh-phrase and the antecedent, whether it is realized on the surface or not, should be preceded by identical prepositions, only the preposition of the antecedent shows up.

(10) apò tēs autēs agnoías hêsper pollà proíesthe tōn koinōn

    by the same want of sense by which you sacrifice many of your interests. (D. 18, 134, in Goodwin, 1025)

We will see later on another way proposed by Bresnan and Grimshaw to account for the absence of one preposition in (5)a-b. Cases like (5)c were accounted for by adopting Emonds' convention (1976) that a sentence with an empty Δ in surface structure, where the Δ hasn't been filled at any point in the derivation, is marked as ungrammatical. We thus assumed that there was no rule deleting the empty antecedent.

Let us turn to cases like (6) now. In Hirschbühler (1976a: 144-145) we said that *là* and *où* could be considered as Adverb Phrases (or reduced Prepositional Phrases) or as Locative NP's. Since *habiter* can take *là/où* as a complement while *acheter* cannot, as can be seen from the following examples, wh-raising could apply in the case of

(6)a but not in the case of (6)b, which we then excluded in the way we did for (5)c:

(11) a. J'habite LÀ où il habite.

I live there where he lives.

b. OÙ habite-t-il?

Where does he live?

(12) a. *J'ai acheté LÀ OÙ il habite.

I bought there where he lives.

b. *Où a-t-il acheté?

*Where did he buy?

(There is a reading of (6)b, (12)a-b, which is grammatical but irrelevant here, with *acheter* meaning *faire des achats* (go buying).)

So, all the facts that we have seen could be accounted for easily by assuming that in free relatives the wh-word occupied the antecedent position in surface structure, that the antecedent was empty in deep structure, that there was a rule of wh-raising and a rule deleting identical prepositions in some environment, and by adopting Emonds' convention on unfilled Δ's. Under the hypothesis that in free relatives in French the wh-word is in the   position, a constraint of the type of (13) is necessary:

(13) [[[[wh W_1] -WH] W_2] W_3]
     $\overline{\overline{X}}_1$ $\overline{S}$ COMP $\overline{\overline{X}}_2$

→ *, if X_1 and X_2 don't match in features.

The -WH feature in   is to ensure that the constraint applies to free relatives only, and not to indirect questions, if, as argued by Bresnan and Grimshaw, they have the $\overline{S}$ dominated by NP. The problem with a constraint like (13) is that it is unclear why it would exist. The facts follow easily however under the assumption that in free relatives the wh-word is in the antecedent position in surface structure. We will now turn to the analysis given by Bresnan and Grimshaw.

7.2 Bresnan and Grimshaw's analysis

The main features of Bresnan and Grimshaw's analysis of free relatives that are relevant for our discussion are:

(a) The wh-word is generated as the head of the free relative in deep structure.

(b) Free relatives in English (and French) are generated by a phrase structure rule like (14)a, while relative clauses headed by a non-wh-phrase are the result of the application of a rule like (14)b:

(14) a. XP → XP S

  b. XP → XP $\bar{S}$

where X is N, Adj, Adv, Prep for English (and N, P for French).

(c) The gap in the free relative is accounted for by a rule of Controlled Pro Deletion (Bresnan and Grimshaw, 1978: 59)

$$XP \ldots XP \ldots \rightarrow XP_i \ldots [_{XP} \ e \ ] \ldots$$
$$[Pro] \qquad\qquad\quad [Pro]_i$$

This rule deletes the terminal string of a pro-category and coindexes the pro-category node with the antecedent node (Bresnan and Grimshaw:58).

(d) The Pro-categories in English are NP, AP, AdvP, PP [+Loc], PP [+Dir], PP [+Temp]. They assume that French has a general PP pro-category, besides NP.

I won't give the details of the arguments for each claim, for which I refer the reader to their very interesting article, but I will quickly review the main arguments.

(a) The wh-phrase is generated in the head position.

  1. accounts for the matching effect (facts concerning pied-piping fit here)

2. accounts for number agreement between a free relative subject and the verb. I don't think this argument goes through, because the same agreement facts are found in languages where it is clear that in free relatives the wh-phrase is in Comp. (Ancient Greek and Middle French for example.)

3. It explains why free relatives are not subject to the NP over S constraint (Kuno, 1973; Bresnan and Grimshaw, 1978, Section 1).

(b) Free relatives are generated by "XP → XP S"

This rule accounts for the absence of a complementizer in free relatives, i.e. for the absence of *that*.

(c) Pro-categories and Controlled Pro Deletion.

The assumption that only locatives, directional, and temporal PP's are pro-PP categories in English, together with the assumption that PP can be the head of a free relative, accounts for the following sorts of contrasts:

(15) a. I'll move to whatever town you move.

b. *I'll talk to whoever she talks.

In the a case there is a pro-directional PP in deep structure, and the head is a directional PP. The rule of Controlled Pro-deletion can apply. In the b case, there is no pro-PP for the sort of PP that the complement of *talk* is. It is thus not possible to have a PP gap there.

Since Bresnan and Grimshaw assume that there is a general Pro-PP category in French, they predict the existence of cases like (5)a-b. (5)a would be derived from (16) by Controlled Pro-deletion.

(16) [je le dis [[pour qui] [je dois le dire [Pro]]]]
                PP PP   S   PP

7.3 Evidence for wh in Comp

We will now examine some facts of Dutch that lead to the conclusion that in that language the wh-phrase in free relatives occupies the Comp position although the matching effect must hold in that language. The conclusion from this is that the matching effect can't be a decisive test for deciding between the two analyses in general. Facts from French and Montreal French will be examined which fit very well with the hypothesis that the wh-phrases in the free relatives of these languages occupy the Comp position although they conform to the matching effect.

7.3.1 Dutch

The following argument is due to Van Riemsdijk (1978). Dutch is an SOV language with extraposition of S̄ but no heavy NP shift. Consider then (17)a and (17)b, where extraposition hasn't applied yet and which sound uncolloquial to all speakers:

(17) a. Jan heeft het geld dat hij had gestolen teruggegeven.

John has the money that he had stolen given-back.

b. Jan heeft wat hij had gestolen teruggegeven.

John has what he had stolen given-back.

Application of extraposition gives (18), which is the standard form:

(18) a. Jan heeft het geld teruggegeven dat hij had gestolen.

John has the money given back that he had stolen.

b. Jan heeft teruggegeven wat hij had gestolen.

John has given back what he had stolen.

That (18)b is not the result of a rule of heavy NP shift is shown by the ungrammaticality of (19), where the whole direct object NP is moved: if there was a rule of heavy NP shift, the result should be grammatical:

(19) *Jan heeft teruggegeven het geld dat hij had gestolen.

We may conclude with Van Riemsdijk that in (17)b, and in (18)b, the wh-phrase is in Comp and not in the antecedent position.

What is particularly interesting then is that free relatives in Dutch obey the matching constraint. So we have:

(20) a. Jan heeft teruggegeven wat hij gestolen had.

John has given back what he had stolen.

b. *Jan heeft teruggegeven op wat jij gezeten had.

John has given back what you sat on.

(21) a. Jan heeft de kerel ontmoet met wie jij gesproken had.

John has met the guy to whom you spoke.

b. *Jan heeft ontmoet met wie jij gesproken had.

John met (him) to whom you spoke.

(22) a. Ik zal het huis kopen waar jij inwoont.

   I will buy the house that you are living in.

b. *Ik zal kopen waar jij inwoont.

   I will buy (the place) where you live.

Such facts have recently been used as evidence to show that in Dutch free relatives the wh-phrase is in the antecedent position (Daalder, 1977). Obviously only one of the analyses is correct. I consider Van Riemsdijk's argument really compelling. Assuming that in Dutch free relatives the wh-phrase is in Comp we can still account for the matching effect by a constraint like (13), or more interestingly, as proposed by Van Riemsdijk (1978), by assuming that in some languages, the COMP position of free relatives must satisfy the strict subcategorization and selectional restriction requirements of the relevant V or P of the matrix clause. If we adopted the other analysis, with the wh-phrase in the antecedent position, we would be at a loss to explain in a satisfactory way the facts uncovered by Van Riemsdijk. One important consequence of this is that the matching effect can no longer be used as evidence in favor of an analysis of free relatives with the wh-phrase occupying the antecedent position; it is merely compatible with such an analysis. The main argument for the analysis proposed by Bresnan for English, Hirschbühler for French, and Bresnan and Grimshaw for English again thus disappears. We turn now to facts from French which we haven't discussed previously and which may lend support to the view that in French the wh-phrase in free relatives occupies the Comp position.

7.3.2 *Quoi* in free relatives

The distribution of *quoi* in free relatives is similar to that found in the case of questions. Consider the following examples:

(23) a. *J'ai acheté quoi tu as acheté.

   I bought what you bought.

b. *J'ai acheté quoi traînait sur la table.

   I bought what was lying on the table.

(24) a. *Je me suis assis sur quoi tu as acheté.

   I sat on what you bought.

b. *Je me suis assis sur quoi se trouvait dans le coin.

   I sat on what was in the corner.

In those examples, *quoi* corresponds to an NP gap, and the result is ungrammatical just as an unmodified fronted *quoi* corresponding to an NP gap is ungrammatical in the case of questions. Just as in questions, replacing *quoi* by *que* or *qui* (intended as corresponding to inanimates) is ungrammatical too. Consider PP gaps now.

(25) a. Je me suis assis sur quoi tu t'es assis.

I sat on what you sat (on).

b. Pierre a caché son argent sous quoi Jacques avait caché le sien.

Peter hid his money under what Jacques hid his (under).

c. Je me suis soigné avec quoi le médecin m'avait dit de me soigner.

I healed myself with what the doctor told me to heal myself (with).

d. Si Jacques essaye de sauter au-dessus de quoi Pierre a sauté, il va se rompre le cou.

If Jacques tries to jump over what Peter jumped (over), he will break his neck.

The judgments on those examples vary from grammatical to uncertainty as to their status, but they are always considered as much better than examples (23) and (24). Let us see now how it is possible to account for these facts.

7.3.2.1 Wh-phrase in COMP

Consider (25)a again:

(25) a. Je me suis assis sur quoi tu t'es assis.

After wh-movement and deletion of the complementizer *que*, the relevant part of the underlying structure of (25)a will be (26).

(26) [sur[[[sur quoi]][tu t'es assis [e]]]]
       PP   NP $\bar{S}$ Comp PP$_i$ S   PP$_i$

The second preposition can then be deleted. I think it is irrelevant whether the PP node in COMP is pruned or not; I will assume it is (interpretation is assumed to be done before deletion). We can then explain why (25) is grammatical and (23) and (24) are not in a way similar to that we used to account for the distribution of *quoi* in questions, though a few reformulations of constraints will be necessary. Remember that we suggested two ways to exclude sentences like (27).

(27) *Quoi as-tu fait?
What did you do?

1. One way was to have an optional rule like (28) plus a filter like (29) (see (103) and (104) in Chapter VI; we omit *diable*).

(28) <u>Quoi/Que rule</u> (optional)

$$[\#QUOI\#] \rightarrow \emptyset\ 2\ \emptyset$$
Comp
    1 2   3

(29) <u>Quoi-filter</u>

$$* [\ \text{quoi}\ ]\ (NP)\ V$$
COMP   [+finite]

Once the proposition in (26) is deleted, and general conventions on word boundary deletions (see Chapter VI, (74)) and rule (28) have applied, we get (30); filter (29) can then apply and mark (30) as ungrammatical.

(30) [sur [[[quoi]][tu t'es assis]]]]
     PP   NP S̄ Comp NP   S

One way to prevent this from happening is to assume that complements of prepositions are marked [+Oblique] while other NP's are marked [-Oblique]. (Depending on the details of the analysis the moment where the marking occurs may be relevant. i.e. before wh-movement, or after wh-movement but before preposition deletion.) Then (28) and (29) can be reformulated as in (30) and (31) so that they apply only to [-Oblique] *quoi*'s.

(31) <u>Quoi/Que rule II</u> (optional)

$$[\ \# QUOI \#\ ] \rightarrow \emptyset\ 2\ \emptyset$$
Comp [-Obl]
    1   2   3

(32) <u>Quoi-filter II</u>

$$*[\ \ \text{quoi}\ \ ]\ (NP)\ V$$
COMP [-Obl]   [+finite]

As the result of the application of (31), the variant *que* will be chosen so that (33) will be generated rather than (23)a:

(33) *J'ai acheté que tu as acheté.

Such examples can be excluded by the surface structure constraint (34) which we already proposed in the preceding chapter to account for the agrammaticality of indirect questions like (35) and indirect exclamatives like (36)a and (36)b:

(34) A structure of the form [...[que...]...] is marked as
$$ S \quad \bar{S}$$
ungrammatical, unless *que* is a complementizer.

(35) *Je me demande que tu as acheté.
I wonder what you bought.

(36) a. *C'est extraordinaire que de chevelus sont arrivés!
It's extraordinary, how many long haired people have arrived!

b. *C'est extraordinaire que de trésors on a perdus!
It's extraordinary how many treasures we lost!

II. The other way we suggested to account for questions like (27) involved a rule deleting word boundaries around *QUOI* in the case stipulated in rule (37) ((100) in chapter VI):

(37) <u>Que-1</u> (Obligatory)

[# QUOI #]   (NP)   V   → ∅ 2 ∅ 4 5
   Comp   [+finite]
   1   2   3   4   5

We would just need to modify it by specifying that *quoi* must be [-Oblique]. When it applies, the allomorph *que* is chosen and the result is excluded by (34). The assumption that the wh-phrase in free relatives in French is in Comp allows us to capture very naturally one aspect common to indirect questions, indirect exclamations, and free relatives. Let us see now what is necessary to account for these facts under the hypothesis that the wh-phrase is in antecedent position.[1]

7.3.2.2 Wh in the antecedent position

We have seen that the wh-phrase could be in the antecedent position either because it is introduced there by the rules of lexical insertion, as Bresnan and Grimshaw do, or because the wh-phrase was raised from the Comp position, as we suggested. I don't think that for the point we are discussing it makes a difference which variant is chosen, and I will assume Bresnan and Grimshaw's approach. One difference between Bresnan and Grimshaw's approach and mine was that the one I suggested allowed us to account for the absence of the complementizer by applying *que*-deletion before wh-raising.

Bresnan and Grimshaw make a distinction between PP heads and NP heads. The ungrammatical cases are those with NP heads, i.e. those where the gap in the embedded clause is an NP gap. It is then possible to account for the ungrammatical cases by a variant of the filter (32) which was part of one possible way to account for the distribution of *quoi* in questions and in free relatives. The modified filter would be:

(38) Quoi-filter III
   *[quoi (NP) V   ...]
           [+finite]

In the case of questions, because of the outside brackets, this will exclude only the cases where the wh-phrase in Comp is *quoi*. In the case of free relatives, it would eliminate only these cases where the antecedent is an NP: *quoi* forms a constituent with the following S (or S̄). If we don't have PP heads, then it seems that we will have to mention that the ungrammatical cases are those where the gap in the embedded sentence is an NP gap, rather than a PP gap, for example by a condition like (39):

(39) * quoi$_i$ [... [e] ...]
         S   NP$_i$

where the main verb of S is in a finite tense.

The specification that no material separates *quoi* from S is necessary so that questions like (40) in standard French and concessive clauses like (41) not be excluded:

(40) a. Quoi que tu n'aimes pas Pierre a-t-il acheté?
       What that you don't like did Peter buy?

   b. Qui pense à quoi que Pierre a acheté?
       Who is thinking about what that Peter bought?

(41) Quoi que tu fasses, je m'en fous.
     Whatever you do, I don't care.

Notice that under the hypothesis that the wh-phrase was in Comp, the second account we considered didn't require any filter mentioning *quoi*: a [-Oblique] QUOI in a Comp of a tensed clause is realized as *que*, and constraint (34), which is already needed, takes care of the ungrammatical cases. This sort of account is unavailable under the hypothesis that the wh-phrase is in the antecedent position.

Although the distribution of *quoi* seems to be of the sort that might help choose between the competing analyses, we are unable to arrive at a strong conclusion in favor of the hypothesis that the wh-phrase is in Comp. What is needed here is a real theory of surface structure constraints along the lines first proposed by Perlmutter (1971), i.e. when is this sort of device necessary and what are possible surface structure constraints, or, if one wants to adopt the sort of theory suggested by Chomsky and Lasnik in "Filters and Control", a restrictive theory of filters. If we want to maintain that surface structure constraints should be used only when no other satisfying solution is available, then we should account for the distribution of *quoi* in free relatives and in questions by adopting the analysis making use of rule (37), plus the constraint (34), an approach that does not seem available if the wh-phrase is in the antecedent position.

7.3.3 Montreal French

The following examples, from Niéger (1976) are grammatical in Montreal French and in some non-standard continental dialects. I accept (42)a,b; I consider (42)d at the limit of grammaticality and (42)c is ungrammatical for me.

(42) a. J'aime QU'EST-CE QUI est bon.

   I like what is good.

 b. Je crois QU'EST-CE QUE Jean m'a dit.

   I believe what Jean told me.

 c. Je mange tout QU'EST-CE QUE je veux.

   I eat everything I want.

 d. J'habite OÙ EST-CE QUE les deux rivières se rencontrent.

   I live where the two rivers meet.

Informants also report the following judgments on sentences not discussed by Niéger; I share these judgments with them.

(43) a. Je me suis assis sur QU'EST-CE QUE tu as acheté.
   I sat on what you bought.

   b. *Je me suis assis sur QU'EST-CE QUE tu t'es assis.
   I sat on what you sat on.

In short, *qu'est-ce que* is good when it corresponds to an NP gap, and it is bad when it corresponds to a PP gap; exactly the same distribution is found in questions, and it is just the distribution opposite to that of *quoi*:

(44) a. Je me demande qu'est-ce que tu as acheté.
   I wonder what you bought.

   b. *Je me demande sur qu'est-ce que tu t'es assis.
   I wonder on what you sat.

The correct analysis of *qu'est-ce que*, *qu'est-ce qui* is still to be given. Some proposals are made by Langacker (1972, 1965), Roulet (1969), and Obenauer (1977). Langacker and Obenauer derive these expressions as the interrogative counterparts of non-interrogative cleft constructions, i.e. *c'est quoi que*, *c'est quoi qui*, and they assume that the result is lexicalized, idiomatized in some way; Obenauer actually assumes that those strings are reanalyzed as NP's. They don't have anything of substance to say about reanalysis and idiomatization rules, but nobody else has either. What is bothersome if these expressions are derived from cleft sentences is how the order between *ce* and *est* is arrived at in the case of embedded questions and free relatives, since subject clitic inversion occurs only in main clauses under some conditions. Roulet assumes the existence of a morpheme ESK, with the allomorphs *est-ce que* and *est-ce qui*. Such a morpheme would have to be sentence initial and if it is a complementizer heading some wh-clauses we could explain why there is no inversion of *tu* for example in (45), since there is no subject clitic inversion when there is a complementizer in Comp, as shown by (46) and (47).

(45) a. *Qui est-ce que as-tu rencontré?

   b. Qui est-ce que tu as rencontré?
   Who did you meet?

(46) a. Où qu' tu vas?

   b. *Où que vas-tu?
   Where are you going?

(47) a. Peut-être est-il malade.
   b. Peut-être qu'il est malade.
   c. *Peut-être qu'est-il malade.
   Maybe he is sick.

In the dialect with *est-ce que/qui*, this complementizer would be allowed to cooccur with a wh-phrase in Comp.

There are problems with all the analyses, but they all have in common that in questions either what precedes *est-ce que/qui* is in Comp, or *est-ce que/qui* plus the wh-phrase that precedes it are in Comp. Whichever approach is chosen, it seems that it could be readily extended to free relatives, and it is then no surprise that *qu'est-ce que* and *qu'est-ce qui* in free relatives are good exactly where they are good in direct and indirect questions, i.e. when the gap in the relative clause is a NP gap (rather than a PP gap). In the analysis with the wh-phrase in the antecedent position, either *que* would have to be in the antecedent position, or *qu'est-ce que/qui* would have to. If only *que* is in the antecedent position, the distribution of the allomorph *que* of the morpheme QUOI would have to be complicated. In addition to saying that *que* is the allomorph chosen in the environment (48)a for questions, it would be necessary to also say that it is chosen in the environment described in (48)b for free relatives.

(48) a. [--------]
        COMP

   b. [------S]

The outside brackets in (48)b ensure that *que* controls an NP position in the embedded sentence. (43)b will then be out because of one of the following reasons. Either we have a PP head, i.e. [sur QUOI], and in that case QUOI doesn't form a constituent with the following S, and so the allomorph must be *quoi*, and (43)b won't be generated. Or, if we have a NP head, so that the chosen allomorph will be *que*, the PP gap in the sentence will not be controlled by a PP and the result will thus be ill-formed. Exactly the same sort of thing would be necessary for *qui est-ce que*, *qui est-ce qui* if some restructuring takes place that makes a derived lexical item out of them. In fact the restructuring is necessary so that examples like (42)a, b, (43)a, and (44)a will not be excluded by a constraint similar to (34). If *que* in free relatives is in the antecedent position, then (34) should be replaced by a constraint like (49):

(49) A structure of the form [... [que S] ...] is marked
          S
ungrammatical unless *que* is the complementizer.

In the case of questions and exclamatives the first brackets around *que* S will be labelled $\bar{S}$, in the case of free relatives they will be labelled NP.

As in 7.3.2., we can't conclude that the analysis of free relatives with the wh-phrase in COMP is the only one possible. The freedom with which rules can be written allows an account of the facts with the wh-phrase in antecedent position. It seems that for further progress to be made on the problem, we need a much more restricted theory of how rules may be written, as well as a better understanding of the nature of *qu'est qui*, *qu'est-ce que* in questions to start with.

7.4. S versus $\bar{S}$

Bresnan and Grimshaw assume that free relatives are introduced by a phrase structure rule like (50), where X ranges over N,P, Adv.

(50) XP → XP S

The choice of S rather than $\bar{S}$ is made in order to account for the absence of *that* in free relatives in English. It would account for the absence of the complementizer in French too. Another consequence of having S rather than $\bar{S}$, though it is never mentioned in the text, is that not having $\bar{S}$ precludes the possibility of having wh-movement in free relatives and forces an analysis with the wh-phrase in the antecedent position; the gap in the embedded clause would then necessarily be the result of an unbounded deletion rule, a sort of rule that has been the debate of much controversy between Chomsky and Bresnan in the last years (see for example Chomsky's and Bresnan's papers in Culicover, Wasow, and Akmajian (1977)). The arguments for choosing S rather than $\bar{S}$ seem, however, weak to me.

Let us observe first that the absence of a complementizer on the surface has generally not been taken as evidence for the absence of an $\bar{S}$ node. For example, Bresnan herself (1972:49, fn. 4) believes "that all S's, embedded or not, have complementizers; these are deleted from non-embedded S's, obligatorily in English but not in some other languages...". Similarly there are embedded clauses where the complementizer must be absent for the sentence to be grammatical, as is the case for example in (51), where the *that* must be deleted in order for the fixed subject constraint, proposed by Bresnan (1972), not to be violated:

(51) a. Who do you think came?

b. *Who do you think that came?

And the *that* is also absent when there is a Wh-phrase in Comp:

(52) a. The man that you met is here.

b. The man who you met is here.

c. *The man who that you met is here.

It is thus quite possible that the absence of *that* (*que*) in free relatives is due to the obligatory deletion of the complementizer in a specific environment. This environment can't simply be stated in terms of the wh-phrase preceding the complementizer, given the existence of examples such as (53) and parallel English examples, like (54) (adopted from Van Riemsdijk, 1978).

(53) A qui que tu n'aimes pas Pierre a-t-il parlé?

To whom that you don't like did Peter talk?

(54) What people that he once knew came to the party?

Obviously, if the wh-phrase is in Comp in free relatives in English and in French, the absence of the complementizer is normal.

Another relevant fact is that *that* is not impossible in some sorts of free relatives, i.e. in those where the wh-phrase is of the form [wh-ever N] except when that phrase is adjacent to the gap created by relativization. So we have the following oppositions (Bresnan and Grimshaw, 1978:fn. 9):

(55) a. Whatever food THAT there may be in that dusty pantry is probably infested with moth eggs.

b. *Whatever food THAT is edible must be shared.

They assume that the very marginal appearance of *that* in this construction is evidence for the reanalysis of $\bar{S}$ to S. But in fact, the existence of examples like (55)a can be taken as clear evidence that there the wh-phrase is in the antecedent position and that we have $\bar{S}$. The ungrammaticality of (55)b and (56) would then still have to be explained.

(56) *Whatever that there may be in that dusty pantry is probably infested with moth eggs.

It might be instructive at this point to look at other languages. Consider Spanish for example. in Spanish there is a difference depending on whether the wh-phrase is of the wh-ever type or not; the complementizer *que* is retained in the wh-ever type and not in the other one:

(57) a. Quienquiera que venga será bienvenido.

  Whoever comes will be welcome.

 b. Iré adondequiera que me invites.

  I will go wherever you invite me.

 c. Invitaré a quienquiera que tú invites.

  I will invite whoever you will invite.

(58) a. Quien la hace la paga.

  He who does wrong suffers.

 b. Cuanto tengo es tuyo.

  All I have is yours.

 c. Invitaré a quien tú invites.

  I will invite who(ever) you will invite.

And in relatives with a non-wh antecedent, the COMP node is never empty in Spanish:

(59) a. El hombre que conoces está aquí.

  The man that you know is here.

What these examples suggest is that it may be worth considering the hypothesis that in cases like (57) the wh-phrase is in the antecedent position while in cases like (58) it is in Comp position; more generally it is possible that universally quantified wh-phrases are in the antecedent position and that non-quantified wh-phrases are in Comp. If this proves to be correct, it is possible that in English too we should distinguish between two constructions, one with the wh-phrase in COMP, another one with the wh-phrase in the antecedent position.

A look at a difference between standard and non-standard French may be instructive too. We have seen that in Standard French the complementizer doesn't show up in free relatives. It does show up in non-standard French however (Bonnard, 1961:180).

(60) a. Où que j'habite, y a pas l'eau.

  Where I live, there is no water.

(60) b. Adresse-toi à qui que tu veux.

Take contact with whoever you want to.

c. J'fais quoi que je peux. (Richepin, La chanson des Gueux)

I do what I can.

Under the sort of approach suggested by Bresnan and Grimshaw, one of the differences between Standard and non-Standard French is that in Standard French, free relatives would be generated through a rule like (61)a while in non-Standard French we would have a rule like (61)b:

(61) a. XP → XP X

b. XP → XP $\overline{S}$

The wh-phrase would be in the antecedent position in both cases, and *que* would show up in Comp in non-Standard French. It is however not necessary to assume this difference in the base rules of both varieties of French to account for the facts. This difference is also found in questions and in regularly headed restrictive relative clauses, where we have $\overline{S}$, as in the following cases. The a example is Standard French and the b example is non-Standard French.

(62) a. De quoi t'occupes-tu?

b. De quoi que tu t'occupes?

What are you taking care of?

(63) a. Qui est là?

b. Qui qu'est là?

Who is there?

(64) Que fais-tu?

Quoi que tu fais?

What are you doing?

(65) a. La personne à qui j'ai donné votre lettre est malade.

b. La personne à qui que j'ai donné votre lettre est malade.

The person to whom I gave your letter is ill.

For other examples of the b kind, see Bonnard (1961, a,b) and references cited therein. Once again, if the wh-phrase is in Comp in free relatives, the distribution of *que* in free relatives will be accounted for in exactly the same way as it is accounted for in questions and regularly headed relatives.

Another problem with having S rather than $\bar{S}$ as expansion of XP is that it predicts the existence of sentences like (66), without *que*, in French:

(66) a. *J'ai rencontré le garçon tu as rencontré.

I met the boy you met.

b. *J'ai visité la maison tu voulais acheter.

I visited the house you wanted to buy.

We would have to rule out such sentences by some surface structure constraint distinguishing wh and non-wh antecedents or prevent insertion of a non-wh NP in an NP position when it is the sister of S for example. All this is unnecessary if we don't have a rule such as (61)a.

The conclusion is that the absence of the complementizer in most free relatives in English and in all free relatives in Standard French is not evidence that we have S. Facts from Spanish suggest that it may be worth considering the hypothesis that in some languages one kind of free relative is really a headed relative while the other is really a headless relative.

7.5 Pro-PP heads

We have seen in 7.2 how Bresnan and Grimshaw accounted for the difference between (67)a and b, repeated here:

(67) a. I'll move to whatever town you move.

b. *I'll talk to whoever she talks.

PP can be the head of a relative clause, and there are Pro-PP's for locative, directional, and temporal phrases only. Using the same apparatus, we can then account for the facts involving PP's by assuming that in free relatives in English the head is a pro-category: (67)a can then be described by (68):

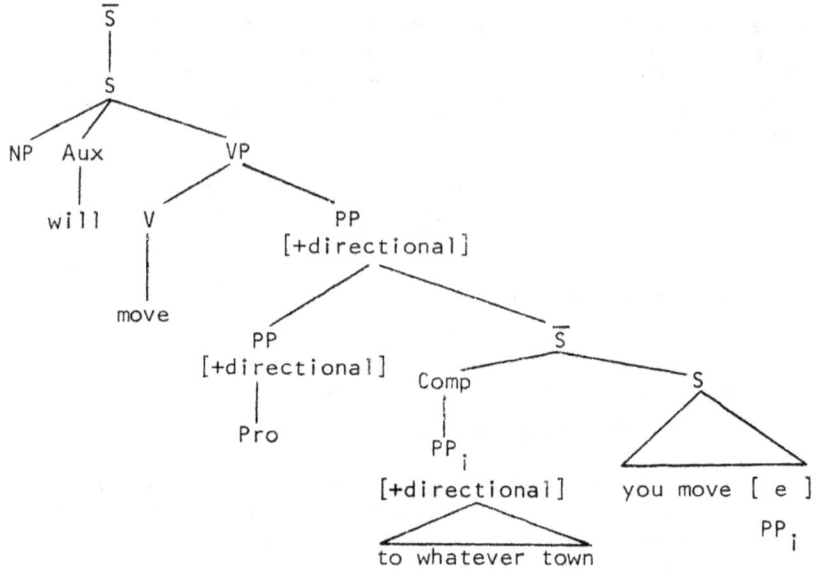

What is needed then is a matching constraint between the pro-head and what is in COMP. Variants can be constructed without a head altogether, with some stipulation as regards directional, locative, and temporal phrases in English. Although one may prefer an analysis without a matching constraint, matching constraints are already necessary to account for free relatives in some languages (as in Finnish (Bresnan and Grimshaw) and in different dialects of German (Van Riemsdijk, 1978)).

My reason for suggesting (68) is not that I believe that this is the way things are, but it is that it is possible to construct alternatives (and probably better ones than that just suggested) to Bresnan and Grimshaw's proposals using some of their insights.

7.6 A first conclusion

Let us conclude the first part of this chapter here. Although there first seemed to be good evidence based on the matching condition for saying that in French, English, and Dutch, the wh-phrase in free relatives occupied the antecedent position, additional facts from Dutch discussed by Van Riemsdijk clearly show that in that language the wh-phrase is in Comp; the matching condition should no longer be used as an argument for saying that in free relatives the wh-phrase occupies the antecedent position. Other facts from Standard French and Montreal (and non-Standard) French fit very naturally with the view that the wh-phrase is in Comp. In discussing the choice of S rather than S̄ for free relatives, we have seen that the absence of a complementizer didn't mean absence of S̄. We have also suggested that it may be worth looking at whether it is not the case that there are two constructions classified as free relatives: one would be a regularly headed relative, where the head would be a quantified wh-phrase, like *quienquiera* in Spanish and *whoever* in English, the other one would be a real headless relative, with a non-quantified wh-phrase.

We have also suggested that the English facts with PP gaps in free relatives could be accounted for by wh-movement in English if we postulated as Bresnan and Grimshaw do that there were Pro-PP's in English only for temporal, locative, and directional complements, and if these pro-PP's could be underlying heads for free relatives.

In the next sections I want to examine a few languages with the wh-phrase in free relatives clearly in Comp.

7.7 Free relatives with wh in Comp.

In this section I want to give examples of languages where it is obvious that in free relatives the wh-phrase is in the Comp position.

7.7.1. Ancient Greek.

Ancient Greek has a rather complex system of relatives and free relatives. For an overview of some aspects of this I refer the reader to Hirschbühler (1976b) and to the references cited therein. The main facts relevant for the present discussion are given below.

1. Headed relatives.

In regularly headed relatives the wh-phrase is in the case required by its function in the embedded clause, except under the following circumstances: if the antecedent is in the genitive or the dative and the wh-phrase should be in the accusative, it takes the case of the antecedent.

7.7.1.1. Headless relatives.

The structural matching effect doesn't obtain in Ancient Greek, as shown by the following examples:

(69) a. eidénai tḕn dúnamin eph hoùs àn íōsin
to discover the strength (*of those*) *against whom*
they are to proceed. (X.A.5.1.8., in Smyth, 2531-a)
for: tḕn dúnamin toútōn eph' hoùs
           gen   acc

(69) b. dià tò avangkaion autoĩs eĩnai dialégesthai par'
hõn láboien tòn misthón

because it is necessary for them to give lessons
to those from whom they expect to receive their
fee. (X.M.1.2.6., in Smyth, 2531-b)

for: toútois par'hõn
       dat   gen

c. eph'hoĩ gàr pleĩsta epónēsan, atelès autoĩs poiḗ seis.

toward what most they tried   you will make for them unattained.

you will undo for them what they tried most to attain.

for: touto eph'hoi

X.Hell, IV, viii,9

d. kaì érōs enépese toĩs pãsin homoíōs ekpleũsai, toĩs
men gar presbutérois hōs ḕ katastrepsoménois *eph'hà*
épleon...

and a desire fell upon all similar to sail, on the
elders as if they would subdue towards what they were
sailing

...and upon all there fell the same desire to sail,
upon the elders as if they were going to subdue the
places they were sailing against...

th., VI, xxiv, 3.

for: tauta eph'ha

Here the free relative occupies an NP position, but the wh-phrase is a PP.

The distribution of cases on the wh-phrases in free relatives is in general parallel to that found in headed relatives and is thus best explained if the wh-phrase is in Comp position. Case attraction is a little more general in free relatives than in headed relatives. In addition to attraction of an accusative wh-phrase into the dative or the genitive, one also finds examples of datives and neuter nominative (phonologically identical to neuter accusative) attracted into the genitive (see Goodwin, 1033). There is no attraction if the wh-phrase is a prepositional phrase. If the free relative is the complement of a preposition and the relativized wh-phrase should start with the same preposition, one of them disappears, the second one we assume, just as in headed relatives (Smyth, 1671). There is no case where the free relative should be complement of a certain

preposition and the wh-phrase is part of a prepositional phrase
whose preposition is different from the first one. Similarly there
is no case where the free relative should be the complement of a
certain preposition and the relative clause starts with a wh-word
which is not in the case required by the preposition. There must
thus be some filter excluding sentences where a free relative complement of a preposition doesn't start with a wh-phrase in the case
required by the preposition.

7.7.1.2. **Internal head relatives.**

Internal head relatives are headless relatives whose wh-phrase
is a regular NP, with at least a wh-word and a noun, and not simply
a wh-word. Either the whole NP appears in Comp, as in (70)a, or
only the wh-word does, as in (70)b; this last situation is by far
the more common:

(70) a. tōn mèn ôun xummáchōn toîs pleístois
of the allies   for most

kaì taîs sitagogoîs holkási kaì toîs ploíois kaì
and for the provision-ships and small boats and

hósē állē paraskeuḕ   xuneípeto próteron
Nom

which-all other armament went with first.

eírēto   es Kérkuran xullégesthai (Th.,6,30,in
was ordered at Corcyre to assemble.   Kühner,332,Rem.14)

Orders had been given beforehand for most of the
allies as well as for the provision-ships and smaller
boats and all the rest of the armament that went
(them) with to assemble at Corcyre.

for: *tēi állēi paraskeuēi   hósē*
Dat   Nom

the other armament   which-all

b. mēd' ... aphélēsthe hūmôn autôn   hḕn dià pantòs aeì
Acc

not   deprive   yourselves (of) which throughout all

to chróno *dóksan* kéktēsthe   *kalḕn*
Acc   Acc

the time fame   you have enjoyed fair. (D.20.
142, in Smyth, 2537-a)

(70) b. Do not deprive yourselves of the fair fame which you have enjoyed throughout all time.

    for: tèn kalèn dóksan hèn
           Acc   Acc
        The fair fame which

It is particularly clear in the case of examples like (70)b which are the most common ones of the two types that the noun is part of the embedded clause, and thus that the wh-word is too. For a discussion of the analysis of these examples, I refer the reader to Hirschbühler (1976b).

Internal head relatives are just a particular case of headless relatives, and as expected they display the same characteristics as free relatives: case attraction is found under the same circumstances (more correctly, I know only of accusatives being attracted, as in headed relatives) and more importantly, no structural matching effect is required, as can be seen from the following examples:

(71) a. ...hupēkoúsate ... *eis hòn* paredóthēte *túpon* didachē̂s
                          Acc   Acc

     you obeyed   *to which* you-were-delivered *form*

     you obeyed that form of teaching which was delivered you. (G.T., Rom.VI,17, in Jelf,p. 546)

     for: *toi túpoi* didachē̂s eis hòn
           Dat   Acc

     that form of teaching which

b. eis dè *hèn* aphíkonto *kṓmēn*   megálē ên
          Acc   Acc

    in   which they arrived village large was

    The village in which they arrived was large (X.A.4.4.2., in Smyth, 2537)

    for: hē kṓmē eis hèn

The first example dates from the end of I A.D. or the beginning of II A.D., while the second is from IV B.C. The two languages have a lot of differences, but the syntax of relative clauses and free relatives didn't change much with respect to the properties that we are interested in. As was the case with (69)a-d, here too the wh-word must be in Comp, since it is made of P+wh-word, and the antecedent would have been an NP.

One last point should be made. Take the last example: the verb of the main clause, ê*n*, is in the third person singular, the person and the number of *hēn kṓmēn*, and the adjective *megálē* is in the feminine singular, the gender of *hēn kṓmēn*, and the case corresponding to the function of the free relative in the main clause, i.e. subject. But there is no surface head. This shows that Bresnan and Grimshaw's argument based on number agreement between a free relative subject and the verb in favor of the wh-phrase being in the head position is without force.

Let us now turn to French from the XIIIth to the XVIth century.

7.7.2. XIIIth-XVIth century French.

We will limit ourselves to giving examples where the wh-phrase is a PP while the whole free relative occupies an NP position, i.e., if there was an antecedent it would be an NP. The wh-phrase must therefore be part of the embedded clause.

(72) a. Et molt par devroit estre liez *Por qui* proier dengneriez.

And very much should be happy (the one) for whom you would deign to pray. (Ren, I, 41, 1446, in Korte, p. 46; XIIIth)

b. Quant il est a Paris venuz Por fere *a quoi* il est tenuz

When he has come to Paris to do (that) to which he has contracted himself. (Rutebeuf, 16, 22, in Korte, p. 90; XIIIth)

(73) Bien aroit pensée torte Ou aveugles les deux yeulx A *qui* il ne plairoit mieulx Q'un bergier.

(She) must have her mind twisted or be blind, (the one) to whom he wouldn't be more pleasing than a shepherd.

(Chr de Pisan, II, 262, 1263, in Korte, p. 46; XIVth)

(74) a. Dieu gard *sans qui* gardé je ne puis estre.

May God protect (the one) without whom I can't be protected.

(Marot, III, 55, in Korte, p. 47; XVIth)

(74) b. Sur ce, je retourneray *dont* j'estoys party.

Things being so, I will go back (there) from where I left.

(Budé, Instit.du Prince, ch. 26, in Huguet, *dont*)

c. Et où diables sont ilz aliez? dis je, car tu n'en as une maille.

-Dont ilz estoyent venuz (dist il).

And where the devil did they go? said I, since you even don't have any of them.

-(There) from where they came.

(Rabelais, II, 17, in Huguet, *dont*)

7.7.3. <u>XVIth-XVIIth century Spanish</u>.

The same sorts of examples can be found in XVIth-XVIIth century Spanish. I gave examples in Hirschbühler (1976a) and additional examples can be found in Bello and Cuervo (1973, 1040), in the *Grámatica de la Lengua Española* of the Real Academia de España(1959, p. 330), and in Keniston (1937, p. 186-193). One difference with the examples seen previously is that here the free relative may be the complement of a preposition and the wh-phrase may also be a prepositional phrase headed by a different preposition:

(75) a. Se rebelo ... contra el servicio *de a quien* se habia ofrecido

He rebelled ... against the service of (the one) to whom he had offered himself.

(Cortes, in Keniston, 15.747)

b. No quería ver más *a con quien* estava.

He no longer wanted to see (the one) with whom he was.

(Theresa de Jesus, id., 15.754)

c. No quiero ver el ceno/Vanamente severo/*De a quien* la sangre ensalza o el dinero.

(Fr. Luis de León, in Bello and Cuervo, p. 335)

Here too, the wh-phrase can't possibly be in the antecedent position.

7.7.4 Present day Spanish.

We will limit ourselves only to tensed clauses here. Spanish offers the interesting features that in some positions the matching condition is violated without problems, as in (76), i.e. with the verb *ser* (be); in subject position it may be violated for some speakers, for more speakers with examples like (77) than with examples like (78). In other positions it seems that the matching condition has to be observed.

(76) a. Tú eres por quien haría todo.

   You are (the one) for whom I would do everything.

b. Pedro es con quien voy a casarme.

   Pedro is (the one) with whom I am going to get married.

(77) a. Con quien salga tendrá que tener un coche.

   (The one) with whom I am going to go out will have to have a car.

b. Con quien me casé se fué.

   (The one) with whom I got married left me.

(78) a. ?Por quien hice todo se fué.

   (The one) for whom I did everything left me.

b. ?Sobre lo que estás sentado me pertenece.

   (That) on what you are sitting belongs to me.

(79) a. *Voy a comprar sobre lo que estás sentado.

   I am going to buy (that) on what you are sitting.

b. *He matado (a) con quien tú saliste.

   I killed (the one) with whom you left.

c. *Con quien te fué me habló ayer.

   (The one) with whom you left talked to me yesterday.

I have not worked on this and the facts should be checked more carefully. I suspect that (76) may be accepted because of its similarity with cleft and pseudo-clefts in Spanish:

(79) d. Es con Pedro con quien voy a casarme.

It is with Peter (with whom) that I am going to get married.

e. Con Pedro es con quien voy a casarme.

Peter is (the one) with whom I am going to get married.

I'll leave the study of these constructions to another time.

7.7.5 A correlation?

I have no explanation for why some languages would be subject to a matching condition in free relatives and others not, or for why some languages would have the wh-phrase in the antecedent position and others not. Excluding present-day Spanish, which on the whole is subject to the condition, a characteristic common to the languages which are not subject to the matching condition is that they may have sentences without surface subject. It is unclear why there could be a relation, but it might be something worth keeping in mind. Another fact is that these languages either had a case system, as Ancient Greek and Old French, and the case on the wh-phrase could clearly show what sentence the wh-phrase was part of (the attraction facts in Greek didn't distinguish headed from headless relatives in general) or they were languages which had not too long ago lost their case system, as Middle French and XVIth century Spanish. In the absence of a case system, in those examples of the sort that don't violate the matching condition, there is no evidence that the wh-phrase is in Comp, and if these sorts of examples were the most frequent, it might have led to a reanalysis whereby the wh-phrase is interpreted as being in the first available slot, i.e. the antecedent position, or to the addition of some filter of the type of (13) in case the wh-phrase is in Comp.

7.8 Infinitival free relatives

I mentioned in Hirschbühler (1976a) that there were some infinitival free relatives in French that don't conform to the matching condition and that are perfect. The example given was:

(80) Il n'a pas où mourir.

He doesn't have where to die.

Another type of example involves *de quoi*:

(81) J'ai de quoi écrire.

I have (things) with which to write.

In (81) it is possible that the *de* is part of the main clause and that a second *de* has been erased, since we have:

(82)　J'ai des crayons.

　　　I have pencils.

In all the examples like (81) there is a paraphrase with a *de + NP*. The gap in the embedded clause can always be paraphrased by *avec + NP* and *de* can generally not be used.

These seem to me the only infinitival free relatives in French that don't obey the matching condition.

Something similar exists in Spanish; consider the following examples (taken from Van Riemsdijk, 1978).

(83)　a.　No tengo con quien bailar.

　　　　　I don't have (anyone) with whom to dance.

　　　b.　No tengo a quien escribir.

　　　　　I don't have (anyone) to whom to write.

　　　c.　*No tengo que leer.

　　　　　I don't have anything to read.

　　　d.　*No tengo a quien matar.

　　　　　I don't have anybody to kill.

If *a quien* in (83)d is bad we should assume, with Van Riemsdijk, that it is an NP, contrary to what is the case in (83)b; in (83)a-b the wh-phrase must be in Comp, and we may assume that it is the case in (83)c-d also. Van Riemsdijk suggests that c and d be excluded because they violate the NP-to-VP filter from Chomsky and Lasnik (1977), which would have to be reformulated so as to be universal:

(84)　*[$_a$ NP-to-VP], unless a is adjacent to and in the

　　　domain of [-N]

Van Riemsdijk's work being still in progress, I will not quote him anymore and hope that it will become available in the near future. Let us mention that my informants accept (83)d. Adopting the NP-to-VP filter, we simply have to assume that *a quien* is what it looks like, i.e. a PP.

One thing on which I would like to insist is that there is clearly a difference between free relatives in a finite tense and infinitival free relatives in Spanish, and that if it appears that the matching condition can always be violated in the case of infinitival free relatives, so that it is clear that the wh-phrase is always in the Comp position in that type of sentence, no conclusion can be drawn from that fact about the right analysis of free relatives in tensed clauses.

7.9 Conclusion

The first point I would like to make is that the variations we have observed between languages with respect to the structural matching condition, or within the same language between infinitival and non-infinitival free relatives, should be a warning not to use indiscriminately facts from one language to support an analysis presented as the correct analysis of free relatives in another language: Bresnan and Grimshaw mention Quicoli (1972) as one of those who have argued for the traditional analysis of free relatives, i.e. with the wh-phrase in Comp, and they argue against that traditional analysis; but Quicoli worked on Greek, and he was right (though he didn't mention the facts violating the matching condition). Similarly, the facts from Greek can't be used to argue against the analysis presented by Bresnan and Grimshaw in the case of languages like English, French, Dutch, and most of Spanish today.

Another question is whether there is evidence suggesting that in these languages the wh-phrase is in Comp also. Van Riemsdijk's argument based on extraposition in Dutch (section 7.3.1) is such an argument for that language and makes it necessary to account for the matching condition in this language by a constraint like (13) or by something else which would have the same result. The facts from Dutch can be used to make points about French, English, or Spanish because they are of the same type. The fact that a constraint like (13) or some principle involving COMP is required for Dutch no longer makes it look like an ad hoc device for those other languages, especially if it is a universal principle that would take effect only in languages with such or such a property, i.e. if it could be independently predictable what sort of languages would conform to it.

Another problem that has come up time and time again in this chapter is that of filters. There is very little that they can't do. Until a theory of filters is developed, there are a certain number of cases where they won't help us decide between analyses, even though one may have the feeling that the facts, such as, for example, those involving *quoi* in free relatives in French, are of the sort that would help choose between analyses.

Other problems have been discussed, about which I have no more to say, for example that of PP head, and that of the absence of the complementizer in free relatives in several languages. Just as all the others, they deserve more investigation, especially the one concerning the complementizer and the use of S versus S̄.

FOOTNOTE TO CHAPTER VII

1. [Addition, Spring 1979] Since writing this, it has become clear that Van Riemsdijk's suggestion that in some languages the COMP of free relatives must be available for strict subcategorization and selectional restrictions of a matrix V or P is enough to account for the grammaticality of examples like (25). So (25)a would be represented as in a, with parentheses indicating that the nodes surrounded by them are perhaps absent.

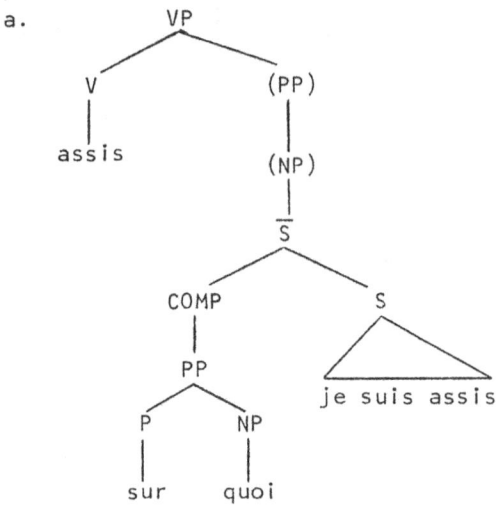

This seems to me to be the correct solution. For a discussion, see Hirschbühler, *La Syntaxe des relatives independantes*, to appear in a volume dedicated to Professor Jacques Pohl (1979).

CHAPTER VIII

CONCLUSION

In these concluding lines I will briefly recapitulate the main results that have been reached in the preceding chapters, indicate some of the remaining questions that seem to me worthy of further research, and make some remarks of a more general character.

In chapters II to IV we have considered three proposals about the meaning of questions. Hausser and Zaefferer (1976) treat direct questions as denoting "sets containing ordered sequences of their questioned elements" (Hausser, 1978:209); Hausser (1978) argues that indirect questions are open sentential complements, and Karttunen (1978a,b) analyzes both direct and indirect questions as denoting sets of true propositions. Hausser's analysis of indirect questions is clearly inadequate and I having nothing more to say about it. We have extended Hausser and Zaefferer's analysis to indirect questions. This analysis and Karttunen's face different problems. I won't speculate on how important and damaging for each approach these problems may turn out to be and leave it to future research to tell us whether they can be overcome or whether still other analyses are preferable. The two analyses have some features in common, one of which seems particularly interesting to me. In both cases, it is necessary to adopt some version of the performative analysis in order to account for the meaning of (1)a paraphrased by (1)b:

(1) a. What grade does every student deserve?

b. For every student, what grade does he deserve?

The discussion in 2.2.1. makes it clear that in the logical framework adopted in chapters II to IV, any semantic analysis of questions that treats them as expressions of some type other than t will have to adopt some version of the performative analysis in order to account for the meaning of (1)a paraphrased in (1)b. The performative analysis has often been criticized on both syntactic and semantic grounds, and the fact that the analyses considered here require the adoption of such an analysis is likely to make the analysis suspicious to many people. It is however incumbent now on those who reject the performative analysis to propose an analysis of questions detailed enough so that we can see whether it accounts, for example, for the different meanings of (1)a. This leads us to some observations on Chomsky's treatment of questions and on May's (1974) account of the ambiguity of questions like (1)a. Chomsky (1977) suggests that questions be represented at the level of logical form with the help of some quantifier. So, (2)a would essentially be represented as in (2)b:

(2) a. Who did John see?

b. For which *x*, *x* a person, John saw *x*

Within Chomsky's theory, logical forms are syntactic objects that still remain to be interpreted (Chomsky and Lasnik, 1977:429), and since no well defined semantics is offered, it is impossible to tell how (2)b is to be interpreted. The consequences of this become particularly clear in May's account of the ambiguity of (1)a. May's treatment of questions is similar to Chomsky's in scope and depth: he offers logical forms but no explicitly defined semantics (though in both cases it is assumed that the apparatus of predicate calculus may be enough to interpret logical forms), in particular, no explicitly defined semantics is given for questions. May hopes to account for the ambiguity of (1)a simply by manipulating *what grade* and *every student*, having one c-commanding the other in logical form and vice versa, assuming that different hierarchical relations in logical forms will necessarily yield different meanings. We have however seen in 2.2.1. that introducing *what grade* and *every student* in different orders with respect to each other (which, in the framework considered there, is the equivalent of having different hierarchical relations in logical forms) does not necessarily determine different meanings. Depending on what meaning questions will be assigned, the two different logical forms proposed by May for questions like (1)a may or may not yield different meanings, but in the absence of some concrete proposal as to how questions are interpreted, there is no way to evaluate May's proposal. One may then ask what is the point of giving a purported disambiguated representation in an uninterpreted notation. More generally, no really testable proposal for the ambiguity of (1)a or for any other question presently exists in the approach taken by Chomsky and May. Whatever the future of the analyses discussed here, they have the merit of being explicit enough to provide a basis for further work.

Very little needs to be said about chapter V. The discussion there shows that iterated multiple questions such as (3) are ambiguous, as most people have assumed.

(3) Who knows where we bought what?

Continued work in this area will probably be fruitful for arriving at a satisfying explanation of why in questions like (4)a the narrow scope reading is bad, as shown by the ungrammaticality of (4)b, and why an unmoved wh-phrase may not make up a multiple question with a clefted wh-phrase, as shown by (5) (I don't consider here the echo-question interpretation of (5)):

(4) a. Who remembers how to interpret which of these formulas?

b. *Peter remembers how to interpret which of these formulas.

(5) *Who is it that bought what?

In chapter VI we have examined the alternation between *que* and *quoi* in questions in French and we have argued, against Obenauer, that *que* in questions is a pronoun rather than a complementizer. Although I have no doubt about the correctness of the position I have defended, many details of the analysis will probably have to be changed once we gain a better understanding of the relations between syntax, morphology, and lexical insertion.

In chapter VII, we have discussed free relatives. It is undoubtedly the case that in languages like Classical Greek, and Old and Middle French the wh-phrase is in Comp position in free relatives. It has been argued by various people that in languages like French, English, and Dutch for example, the wh-phrase actually occupies the antecedent position in free relatives. The situation in Dutch shows however that what was thought of as strong evidence in favor of this, i.e. the fact that these languages obey 'the matching condition', is no longer any evidence at all for that position. What is more interesting to me than the controversy about the position of the wh-phrase itself is whether it is possible to predict from some other aspect of a language if it will display the matching effect. This should eventually lead to an explanation of why some languages like French at one time didn't exemplify the matching condition while later they started to.

As far as the semantics of free relatives is concerned, which should be similar to that of definite or generic NP's, depending on the context, I see no difficulty in accounting for it whether we have the wh-phrase in the antecedent position or in Comp. There is thus no way to decide between the competing syntactic analyses of free relatives for languages like French and English on semantic grounds. Concerning the much more general problem of the input to the interpretive rules -- is it surface structure or as in the original version of Montague Grammar, is each syntactic rule paired with a semantic rule (among which we have the identity mapping) --, I believe that presently each position (as well as others) can be defended with good arguments. I have not tried to address this issue directly in this thesis, but it is an area well worth further investigation.

BIBLIOGRAPHY

Academia Española. 1959. *Gramática de la lengua española*. Madrid: Espasa-Calpe.

Allen, C.L. 1977. *Topics in Diachronic English Syntax*. Ph.D. dissertation, University of Massachusetts, Amherst.

Andersson, L. G. 1974. Questions and other open structures. *Logical Grammar Report 9*. (Research Project for Logical Grammar, Department of Linguistics, University of Gothenburg, Sweden).

Andrews, A. 1975. *Studies in the Syntax of Relative and Comparative Clauses*. Ph.D. dissertation, MIT.

Aqvist, Lennart. 1975. *A New Approach to the Logical Theory of Interrogatives*. Tübingen: TBL Verlag Gunter Narr.

Bach, E. 1977. Montague grammar and classical transformational grammar. Ms., University of Massachusetts, Amherst.

Baker, C. L. 1968. *Indirect Questions in English*. Ph.D. dissertation, University of Illinois, Urbana.

Bello, A. and R. Cuervo. 1973. *Gramática de la lengua castellana*. 9th edition. Buenos Aires: ESA.

Bennet, M. R. 1974. *Some Extensions of a Montague Fragment of English*. Ph.D. dissertation, UCLA. Distributed by Indiana University Linguistics Club.

Berthelon, C. 1955. *L'espression du haut degré en francais contemporain; essai de syntaxe affective*. Bern: Francke.

Bolinger, D. 1978. Yes-no questions are not alternative questions. In H. Hiz (ed.), *Questions*. Dordrecht: Reidel, 87-105.

Bonnard, H. 1961. Le systeme des pronoms "qui, que, quoi" en français. *Le français moderne* 29. 168-82, 241-51.

Bresnan, J. W. 1972. *The Theory of Complementation in English Syntax*. Ph.D. dissertation, MIT.

_____. 1973. 'Headless' relatives. Ms., University of Massachusetts, Amherst.

_____ and J. Grimshaw. 1978. The syntax of free relatives in English. *Linguistic Inquiry* 9. 331-91.

Carden, G. 1973. *English Quantifiers: Logical Structure and Linguistic Variation.* Tokyo: Taishukan Publishing Company.

Casagrande, J. and B. Saciuk (eds.). 1972. *Generative Studies in Romance Languages.* Rowley, Mass: Newbury House.

Chomsky, N. 1973. Conditions on transformations. In S. R. Anderson and P. Kiparsky (eds.), *A Festschrift for Morris Halle.* New York: Holt, Rinehart, and Winston.

_____. 1977. On WH-movement. In P. Culicover, T. Wasow and A. Akmajian (eds.), *Formal Syntax.* New York: Academic Press.

_____ and H. Lasnik. 1977. Filters and control. *Linguistic Inquiry* 8. 425-504.

Cooper, R. 1975. *Montague's Semantic Theory and Transformational Syntax.* Ph.D. dissertation, University of Massachusetts, Amherst.

_____. 1978. A fragment of English with questions and relative clauses. Ms. (preliminary version), University of Wisconsin, Madison.

_____ and T. Parsons. 1976. Montague grammar, generative semantics and interpretive semantics. In B. Partee (ed.), *Montague Grammar.* New York: Academic Press.

Daalder, S. 1977. Over relatieve zinnen met ingesloten antecedent. *Spektator* 6-718. 401-07.

Egli, U. 1973. Semantische Repraesentation der Frage. *Dialectica* 27. 363-70.

_____. 1974. *Ansaetze zur Integration der Semantik in die Grammatik.* (Linguistik und Kommunikationswissenschaft, 3) Kronberg: Scriptor.

_____. 1976. *Zur Semantik des Dialogs.* Sonderforschungsbereich 99, Linguistik, Universität Konstanz, W. Germany.

Ehrenkranz, Jean. 1973. Sometimes, OR = AND. *Linguistic Inquiry* 4. 241-42.

Emonds, J. 1976. *A Transformational Approach to English Syntax: Root, Structure-Preserving, and Local Transformations.* New York: Academic Press.

Flynn, M. 1978. VP anaphora and Montague grammar. Ms., University of Massachusetts, Amherst.

Gee, J. 1974. Notes on free relatives. Ms., Stanford University.

Gérard, J. 1977. *La syntaxe de l'exclamation en français*. Thèse de 3ᵉ cycle, Université de Paris VIII/Vincennes.

Goldsmith, J. 1977. Complementizers and the status of root sentences. *Proceedings of the Eighth Meeting of the North East Linguistic Society*, Amherst, Mass.

_____. 1978. 'Que', c'est quoi? 'Que', c'est 'quoi'. Ms., Indiana University.

Goodwin, W. 1892. *A Greek Grammar*, Boston: Ginn.

Gougenheim, G. 1970a. *Etudes de grammaire et de vocabulaire français*. Paris: Editions Picard.

_____. 1970b. Animé et inanimé. A propos de "qui" interrogatif et relatif prépositionnel. In Gougenheim 1970a, 113-23.

_____. 1970c. L'emploi des pronoms interrogatifs "que" et "quoi" devant l'infinitif. In Gougenheim 1970a, 124-29.

Grevisse, M. 1964. *Le bon usage*. 8th edition. Gembloux: J. Duculot.

Grimshaw, J. 1977. *English WH-constructions and the Theory of Grammar*, Ph.D. dissertation, University of Massachusetts, Amherst.

Gross, M. 1968. *Grammaire transformationnelle du français: syntaxe du verbe*. Paris: Larousse.

Haase, A. 1969. *Syntaxe française du XVIIe siècle*. Paris: Delagrave.

Hamblin, C.L. 1973. Questions in Montague English. *Foundations of Language* 10. 41-53.

Hankamer, J. 1974. On WH-indexing. *NELS V: Papers from the Fifth Meeting of the Northeastern Linguistic Society*. Cambridge: Department of Linguistics, Harvard University.

Hausser, R. 1978. *Linguistic Cross-Connections: a formal fragment of English* (Chapter V: The Logic of Questions and Answers, p. 195-247). Institut für Deutsche Philologie, Ludwig-Maximilians Universität, Munich.

Hausser, R. To appear. Surface compositionality and the semantics of mood. In F. Kiefer and J. Searle (eds.), *Speech Act Theory and Pragmatics*. Dordrecht: Reidel.

──────── and D. Zaefferer. To appear. Questions and answers in a context-dependent Montague grammar. In F. Guenthner and S. J. Schmidt (eds.), *Formal Semantics and Pragmatics for Natural Languages*. Dordrecht: Reidel.

Hintikka, J. 1974. Questions about questions. In M. K. Munitz and P. K. Unger (eds.), *Semantics and Philosophy*. New York: New York University Press, 103-58.

──────── . 1976. *The Semantics of Questions and the Questions of Semantics*. Amsterdam: North Holland.

Hirschbühler, Paul. 1976a. Two analyses of free relatives in French. *Papers from the Sixth Meeting of the North Eastern Linguistics Society. Montreal Working Papers in Linguistics*, May 1976, pp. 137-52.

──────── . 1976b. Headed and headless free relatives, a study in French and Classical Greek. Ms., Linguistics Department, University of Massachusetts, Amherst. (To appear in P. Barbaud (ed.), *Les contraintes sur les règles*. Rapport de recherche No. 2, Université du Québec, Montreal.

──────── . 1977. On the non-ambiguity of questions containing multiple questions, or "Who knows why we say what?". Ms., University of Massachusetts, Amherst.

Huddleston, R. and O. Uren. 1969. Declarative, interrogative and imperative in French. *Lingua* 22. 1-26.

Huguet, E. 1925-1966. *Dictionnaire de la langue française du seizième siècle*. 7 vols., Paris.

Hull, R. D. 1974. *A Logical Analysis of Questions and Answers*, Ph.D. dissertation, Cambridge University.

──────── . 1975. A semantics for superficial and embedded questions in natural language. In E. L. Keenan (ed.), *Formal Semantics of Natural Language*. Cambridge: Cambridge University Press, 35-45.

Huot, H. 1974. Les relatives parenthétiques. In Rohrer and Ruwet (eds.) 1974.

Ioup, G. 1975. *The Treatment of Quantifier Scope in a Transformational Grammar*. Ph.D. dissertation, CUNY, Graduate Center.

Jackendoff, R. 1977. $\overline{X}$ *Syntax: A Study of Phrase Structure*, Cambridge: MIT Press.

Jelf, W. 1842-1845. *A Grammar of the Greek Language*. Oxford.

Jensen, J. S. 1973. L'infinitif et la construction relative en français et en italien contemporains. *Revue Romane* 8: 1-2. 122-32.

Jespersen, O. 1974. *The Philosophy of Grammar*. London: Allen and Unwin.

_____. *A Modern English Grammar on Historical Principles* (=MEG). London: Allen and Unwin.

Karttunen, F. and L. Karttunen. 1978. The clitic -kin/-kaan in Finnish. *Texas Linguistic Forum* (Department of Linguistics, University of Texas at Austin) 5. 89-118.

Karttunen, L. 1975. Syntax and semantics of questions. Paper read at the 1975 Winter LSA Meeting.

_____. 1977a. Syntax and semantics of questions. *Linguistics and Philosophy* 1. 3-44.

_____. 1977b. Questions revisited. To appear in *Proceedings of the Albany Conference on Montague Grammar, Philosophy and Linguistics*.

_____ and S. Peters. 1975. Conventional implicatures in Montague grammar. *BLS 1: Proceedings of the First Annual Meeting of the Berkeley Linguistic Society*. Berkeley.

_____, _____. 1976. What indirect questions conventionally implicate. *CLS 12: Papers from the Twelfth Regional Meeting, Chicago Linguistic Society*. Chicago.

Kayne, R. 1972. Subject inversion in French interrogatives. In Casagrande and Saciuk 1972.

_____. 1974. French relative 'que' (Part I). *Recherches Linguistiques* (Université de Paris VIII, Vincennes) 2. 40-61.

_____. 1975a. French relative 'que' (Part II). *Recherches Linguistiques* (Université de Paris VIII, Vincennes) 3. 30-92.

Kayne, R. 1975b. *French Syntax. The Transformational Cycle.* Cambridge: MIT Press.

─────── and J. Y. Pollock. To appear. Stylistic inversion, successive cyclicity, and move NP in French. *Linguistic Inquiry* 9.4.

Keenan, E. L. and R. D. Hull. 1973a. The logical presuppositions of questions and answers. In D. Franck and J. S. Petöfi (eds.), *Präsuppositionen in Philosophie und Linguistik.* Frankfurt: Athenäum, 441-66.

─────── , ───────. 1973b. The logical syntax of direct and indirect questions. In C. Corum, T. Smith and A. Weiser, *You Take The High Node and I'll Take the Low Node: Papers from the Comparative Syntax Festival.* Chicago: Chicago Linguistic Society, 348-71.

Kemp, W. 1977. Noun phrase questions and the question of movement rules. *CLS* 13. *Papers from the Thirteenth Regional Meeting of the Chicago Linguistic Society*, 198-212.

Keniston, H. 1937. *The Syntax of Castilian Prose, The Sixteenth Century*, Chicago: University of Chicago Press.

Klima, E. S. 1964. *Studies in Diachronic Transformational Syntax.* Ph.D. dissertation, Harvard University.

Korte, J. 1910. *Die beziehungslosen Relativsätze im Französischen.* Göttingen.

Kühner, R. 1867. *Grammar of the Greek Language.* New York.

Kuno, S. 1973. Constraints on internal clauses and sentential subject, *Linguistic Inquiry* 4. 363-85.

─────── and J. Robinson. 1972. Multiple WH-questions. *Linguistic Inquiry* 3. 463-87.

Kuroda, S. Y. 1968. English relativization and certain related problems. *Language* 44. Reprinted in D. Reibel and S. Schane (eds.), *Modern Studies in English*, Englewood Cliffs, N.J.: Prentice-Hall.

Langacker, R. W. 1972. French interrogatives revisited. In Casagrande and Saciuk 1972, 36-69.

Lerch, E. 1925. *Historische französische Syntax. I.* Leipzig: Reisland.

Lowenstamm, J. 1977. Relative clauses in Yiddish: a case for movement. *Linguistic Analysis* 2. 197-216.

May, R. 1977. *The Grammar of Quantification.* Ph.D. dissertation, MIT.

McCloskey, J. 1978. *Questions and Relative Clauses in Modern Irish.* Ph.D. dissertation, University of Texas, Austin.

Milner, J. C. 1977. De quelques restrictions limitant le mouvement de qu-. Ms., Université de Paris VII.

Moignet, G. 1974a. *Etudes de psychosystématique française.* Paris: Klincksieck.

───────. 1974b. Le système du paradigme Qui/Que/Quoi. In Moignet 1974a, 163-83.

Montague, R. 1974. The proper treatment of quantification in ordinary English. In R. Thomason (ed.), *Formal Philosophy: Selected Papers of Richard Montague.* New Haven: Yale University Press.

Moreau, M. L. 1970. *Trois aspects de la syntaxe de C'EST.* Ph.D. dissertation, Université de Liège.

───────. 1971. 'L'homme que je crois qui est venu'; *qui, que:* relatifs et conjonctions? *Langue française* 2. 79-90.

Nakada, S. 1976. *Aspects of Interrogatives and Related Phenomena: A Case Study from Japanese and English.* Ph.D. dissertation, University of Michigan.

Obenauer, H. G. 1976. *Etudes de syntaxe interrogative du français.* Quoi, combien, *et le complémenteur.* Tübingen: Niemeyer.

───────. 1977. Syntaxe et interprétation: *que* interrogatif. *Le français moderne* 45. 305-41.

Parsons, T. 1977. Type theory and ordinary language. Ms., University of Massachusetts, Amherst.

Partee, B. H. 1975. Montague grammar and transformational grammar. *Linguistic Inquiry* 6. 203-300.

Partee, B. H. 1976. Semantics and syntax: the search for constraints. In C. Rameh (ed.), *Semantics: Theory and Application*. (Georgetown University Round Table on Languages and Linguistics 1976.) Washington: Georgetown University Press.

Perlmutter, D. 1971. *Deep and Surface Structure Constraints in Syntax*. New York: Holt, Rinehart, and Winston.

Postal, P. 1971. *Cross-over Phenomena*. New York: Holt, Rinehart, and Winston.

Quicoli, C. 1972. *Aspects of Portuguese Complementation*. Ph.D. dissertation, State University of New York, Buffalo.

Rohrer, C. and N. Ruwet (eds.). 1974. *Actes du colloque franco-allemand de grammaire transformationnelle*. Vol. 1. Tübingen: Max Niemeyer.

Roulet, E. 1969. *Syntaxe de la proposition nucléaire en francais parlé: étude tagmémique et transformationnelle*. Bruxelles: Aimav.

Sag, I. 1976. *Deletion and Logical Form*. Ph.D. dissertation, MIT. Distributed by Indiana University Linguistics Club.

Sandfeld, K. 1928. *Syntaxe du français contemporain.I. Les pronoms,* Paris: Champion.

_____. 1936. *Syntaxe du français contemporain. II. Les propositions subordonnées*. Paris: Droz.

Schachter, P. 1973. Focus and relativization. *Language* 49. 19-47.

Selkirk, L. 1972. *The Phrase Phonology of English and French*. Ph.D. dissertation, MIT.

Smyth, H. 1974. *Greek Grammar*. 9th printing. Cambridge: Harvard University Press.

Van Riemsdijk, H. 1978. A note on infinitival free relatives. Ms. (preliminary version), Amsterdam.

Vergnaud, J. R. 1974. *French Relative Clauses*. Ph.D. dissertation, MIT.

Wachowicz, K. 1974. *On the Syntax and Semantics of Multiple Questions*, Ph.D. dissertation, University of Texas, Austin.

Williams, E. 1977. Discourse and logical form. *Linguistic Inquiry* 8. 101-39.

Woolford. To appear. Free relatives and other base generated WH constructions. *Papers from the Fourteenth Regional Meeting of the Chicago Linguistic Society*. Chicago.

For Product Safety Concerns and Information please contact our EU
representative GPSR@taylorandfrancis.com
Taylor & Francis Verlag GmbH, Kaufingerstraße 24, 80331 München, Germany

www.ingramcontent.com/pod-product-compliance
Lightning Source LLC
Chambersburg PA
CBHW052120300426
44116CB00010B/1744